Conversations About Philosophy
Volume 1

Conversations About

PHILOSOPHY

Volume 1

Edited by Howard Burton

Ideas Roadshow conversations present a wealth of candid insights from some of the world's leading experts, generated through a focused yet informal setting. They are explicitly designed to give non-specialists a uniquely accessible window into frontline research and scholarship that wouldn't otherwise be encountered through standard lectures and textbooks.

Over 100 Ideas Roadshow conversations have been held since our debut in 2012, covering a wide array of topics across the arts and sciences.

All Ideas Roadshow conversations are available both as part of a collection or as an individual eBook.

See www.ideasroadshow.com for a full listing of all titles.

Copyright ©2021 Open Agenda Publishing. All rights reserved.

ISBN: 978-1-77170-107-5 (pb)
ISBN: 978-1-77170-108-2 (eBook)

Edited, with preface and all introductions written by Howard Burton.

All *Ideas Roadshow Conversations* use Canadian spelling.

Contents

TEXTUAL NOTE 7

PREFACE 9

APPRECIATING ANALYTIC PHILOSOPHY
A CONVERSATION WITH SCOTT SOAMES

Introduction 17
I. An Analytical Introduction 22
II. Investigating Logic 31
III. Language and Meaning 36
IV. Legal Applications 46
V. Changing the Culture 51
VI. Gödelian Challenges 55
Continuing the Conversation 60

PLATO'S HEAVEN
A USER'S GUIDE
A CONVERSATION WITH JAMES ROBERT BROWN

Introduction 63
I. Introducing Platonism 70
II. Attacks and Defenses 77
III. Seeing With the Mind's Eye 92
IV. Platonism Bounces Back 100
V. The Philosophical Life 107
Continuing the Conversation 117

DEFINED BY RELATIONSHIP
A CONVERSATION WITH CHARLES FOSTER

Introduction 121
I. An Aristotelian Encounter 125
II. Studies in Empathy 132
III. Childhood 138
IV. Engagement 141
V. Dignity 150
VI. Creating Impact 161
Continuing the Conversation 165

PHILOSOPHY OF BRAIN
A CONVERSATION WITH PATRICIA CHURCHLAND

Introduction 169
I. Playing with Brains 174
II. Neuropioneers 179
III. Sociological Fault Lines 184
IV. Connecting Horizontally 190
V. Touching a Nerve 194
VI. Social Relevance 200
VII. Free Will 205
VIII. Eliminative Materialism 209
IX. Consciousness 213
X. Summing Up 218
Continuing the Conversation 221

FREE WILL
AN INVESTIGATION
A CONVERSATION WITH ALFRED MELE

Introduction 225
I. Becoming A Philosopher 229
II. Outlining The Problem 237
III. Neuroscience 253
IV. Social Science 266
V. Next Steps 272
Continuing the Conversation 280

Textual Note

The contents of this book are based upon separate filmed conversations with Howard Burton and each of the five featured experts.

Scott Soames is Distinguished Professor of Philosophy at University of Southern California. This conversation occurred on September 28, 2014.

James Robert Brown is Emeritus Professor of Philosophy at the University of Toronto. This conversation occurred on February 5, 2013.

Charles Foster is a writer, traveller, veterinarian, barrister, philosopher and Fellow of Green Templeton College, University of Oxford. This conversation occurred on October 5, 2016.

Patricia Churchland is UC President's Professor of Philosophy Emerita at UC San Diego and an adjunct professor at the Salk Institute for Biological Sciences. This conversation occurred on April 13, 2014.

Alfred Mele is the William H. and Lucyle T. Werkmeister Professor of Philosophy at Florida State University. This conversation occurred on November 1, 2014.

Howard Burton is the creator and host of Ideas Roadshow and was Founding Executive Director of Perimeter Institute for Theoretical Physics.

Preface

Philosophers, most people will unhesitatingly tell you, spend their days contemplating the "big questions", like how we can be certain of what we know and to what extent humans differ from machines. Often, that is a little more than a cartoon of the real situation: cavalierly ignoring the manifold rigours of what is often a highly technical domain in order to conjure up images of a professional career whose principal requirements involve staring out the window and contemplating the deeper meaning of it all.

But sometimes, it must be admitted, it's not all that far from the mark.

In this collection, we present five examples of precisely such a drilling down into philosophical bedrock, along the way providing a number of highly revealing examples of what high-level philosophical thinking is really all about.

We begin with the longstanding issue of what mathematics actually is and two what extent it is a product of the human mind or has its own independent reality, offering up two rather different perspectives.

On the more formalist side of things, renowned USC analytic philosopher **Scott Soames** points us towards Gottlob Frege's pioneering insights in the latter part of the 19th century.

> "The story of analytic philosophy, in my opinion, really starts in 1879 with a German philosopher named Gottlob Frege. We call him a philosopher, though he was actually in the mathematics department—he was trained in mathematics—and his interest in philosophy began as an interest in the philosophy of mathematics. What is 'the philosophy of mathematics'? Well, he wanted to know what the basic,

mathematical objects are and how the different aspects of the study of mathematics were connected to each other and to non-mathematics.

"To put it very simply, he wanted to know, What are numbers and what is the nature of mathematical knowledge? He came up with answers to both of those questions, which proved to be very influential in the development of logic, mathematics, and philosophy in general. What Frege ended up doing was saying something like this: 'A Natural number is a member of the smallest set that contains zero and is closed under successor.' That is, if you start with something in the set, and you apply successor, you're still in the set. Being the smallest just means that it's a member of every set of which those conditions hold.

"Now that we've got that straight, we can define counting in terms of successors, addition in terms of repeated counting, multiplication in terms of repeated addition, and so forth—thereby building up all of arithmetic. And what did we build it up from? These definitions plus what? Just ordinary, logical reasoning. So the idea is that, if you can formalize logic and address the question ,What is ordinary, logical reasoning?—get a set of axioms and add these definitions, you end up with arithmetic, the theory of the Natural numbers.

"Now, once you have arithmetic, you can define other parts of mathematics in terms of constructions on arithmetic. It's the same approach: you're always taking a higher theory, finding out what its basic, primitive vocabulary is, defining it in terms of the primitive vocabulary of the lower theory, using the axioms of the lower theory to prove the axioms of the higher theory—and now you've reduced the higher to the lower. For Frege, the idea was to reduce all of mathematics to logic..."

University of Toronto philosopher of science **James Robert Brown**, on the other hand, pushes the clock considerably further back, encouraging us to grapple with a longstanding view of the independent metaphysical reality of mathematics that began with Plato and Pythagoras.

"Think of all of the mathematical things that you already believe: two plus three equals five, that there are an infinitude of numbers,

that there are an infinitude of prime numbers, and so on. And then ask yourself, 'Are all those facts, those mathematical facts, are they like physics?'

"*When I say, 'Protons are heavier than electrons,' I'm saying something true about the world, a statement of something that is independent of me, something that's out there that physicists have discovered. Is math like that? Or is it more like this: Bishops move diagonally in the game of chess. That's also true, but it's something that we've obviously created.*

"*So the first question is, Which side are you on? Now, some people opt for the game. They think, Oh, it's an awful lot like a game. And that will give you certainty in mathematics. I mean, it's certain that bishops move diagonally simply because we have agreed that they do. On the other hand, if you think that mathematics is somehow or other out there, waiting; that mathematicians actually make discoveries, just like physicists make discoveries about the world, then you are on the Platonic side of things: mathematics has a kind of independent existence from us.*

"*Another way of putting it is to ask the question, If no conscious beings existed anywhere in the universe, would it still be true that there are infinitely many prime numbers?*"

One of the core problems of mathematical Platonism, as Jim is naturally quick to recognize, is how it's possible for us to actually gain knowledge of this abstract metaphysical realm that necessarily exists outside of time and space. But the question of how we sufficiently ground our mathematical knowledge is hardly the only grand epistemic challenge the world poses to us, as University of Oxford's **Charles Foster**—lawyer, writer, traveller, philosopher, veterinary surgeon and far too many other things to mention—is quick to point out. In particular, Charles concentrates on to what extent we can be certain of what we assume others around us are actually thinking.

"*I grew up in an outer suburb of Sheffield in the North of England. We had a privet hedge around our garden and in one of those privet hedges there lived a blackbird. And that blackbird looked at me with* its yellow eye with a black pupil, and I looked at the blackbird; and what I saw in its beautiful eye enraged and tantalized me, because it plainly knew something about that little suburban garden that I didn't know. I thought I knew it pretty well. And I wondered what it was, and how I could find out what it was. I tried everything I could to try to get inside the head of that blackbird.

"I have been tantalized ever since by the question, What did that creature know of the world? And as I have grown older, I've become tantalized by the question, What do any of us know about the contents of the heads of anything? So, you're looking at me now, and I presume that you are seeing what I see myself: an overweight, balding, middle-aged man, wearing a scruffy grey jacket. But I have no real way of being sure that that's what you're seeing.

"But I have been worried, as I guess we are all worried at some point, whether all my conversations, with even those I think I know best, are conversations at cross-purposes. When I talk to my wife over dinner, are we really agreeing about the basics of the conversation? Do I really know anything at all about what makes my children tick?

"These are the basic epistemological questions; uncertainty about those questions propels people into the insecurities which torment me—and into lots of extremely boring philosophical papers."

UC San Diego **Patricia Churchland**, meanwhile, steadily drifted towards a more biological approach, as her philosophical inquiries increasingly led her to believe that the answers would lie in penetrating the secrets of the human brain—a view that met a surprising amount of resistance from her professional colleagues at the time.

"I was basically in philosophy because I really wanted to understand the nature of knowledge, consciousness, and decision-making. I thought that was what it was all about, except it turned out it wasn't. Instead it was all about words.

"Many people had the view that, even if there is no nonphysical soul, you still cannot ever explain psychological phenomena in neurophysiological terms because the gap is too great. Amongst philosophers there was this idea of what they called "the autonomy *of psychology". What that meant was that you can think of cognition and all that fancy, high-function stuff as software running on the hardware. Now, if you want to understand, say, a word-processing program, you're not going to pay attention to the hardware—so the argument ran—so why should we pay any attention to the brain? You're wasting your time. It's very charming. It's nice that you like it and all of that, but ultimately it's a waste of time.*

"Paul and I were just total outsiders when it came to all that. We were just wasting our time as far as they were concerned. They thought neuroscience was never going to have anything to say about the nature of cognition, while our view was, How can it do anything but?"

Finally, there is Florida State University philosopher **Alfred Mele** who has spent countless professional hours puzzling over age-old philosophical conundrums of free will, self-deception and self-control.

"My first book is called Irrationality, and it's on what's called weakness of will, self-deception and self-control. Aristotle had a view on weakness of will, so did Plato, and they both had views on self-control. Self-deception they didn't have much to say about: Aristotle had nothing that I can think of, while Plato only had one sentence: 'The lie in the soul is the worst thing of all.' That's about it. 'The lie in the soul' is lying to yourself.

"And I wanted to know how it could happen. Weakness of will is a matter of being convinced that it's best to do one thing, but then not doing it and doing something else instead when you could have done the thing that you believed to be best.

"For example, you believe it's best not to have a third bottle of beer because you're about to drive home, but you have one. Or, you believe it's best not to eat a second dessert, but you eat one anyway. Plato actually thought, 'This can't happen unless the guy doesn't really know what's best.' Which means that if you do go ahead and do that then you must either have been compelled to do it or you didn't really know. Aristotle had a more relaxed attitude, but generally speaking he seemed to think that there had to be some defect in your knowledge in order to do this.

"And I just thought, Well, this sort of thing happens all the time. It happens to me. People tell me it happens to them. How does it actually work? And to figure that out, I didn't want to do it just purely hypothetically or purely intellectually. I wanted to look at data. So I did: I looked at lots of data. From quite early on in my career I was really interested in how we could apply scientific findings to these age-old philosophical questions."

Most of "the big questions", then, still remain unanswered. But that hardly means they always will.

Appreciating Analytic Philosophy

A conversation with Scott Soames

Introduction
The Utility of Philosophy

Back in 523, Boethius, the highly erudite and once-mighty advisor to the Ostrogothic King Theodoric the Great, found himself the victim of trumped-up charges of treason by his political enemies, for which he was later tortured and executed. While awaiting trial, however, he took the opportunity to pen what would later become one of the most famous works of the Western literary canon: *The Consolation of Philosophy*.

Aside from detailed ruminations on standard philosophical subjects, such as free will, justice, morality and the existence of evil, Boethius spends considerable time both directly and indirectly addressing the merits of philosophy itself, a meditation made all the more poignant given his current circumstances and imminent fate.

Since personal wealth and political influence are all too transient, he notes coolly, there is little point in feeling sorry for oneself once they evaporate. But the one, true everlasting good is the proper cultivation of one's mind, which is naturally immune to any such external twists of fickle fortune.

This, according to Boethius and scores of his intellectual descendants cascading down throughout the centuries, is the immeasurable consolation that philosophy brings, and thus the principal motivation for turning one's attention to philosophical issues in the first place.

But Scott Soames, one of the world's foremost analytic philosophers and Distinguished Professor of Philosophy at the University of Southern California, looks at things slightly differently. Without diminishing the inherent moral and lifestyle benefits of his field, Scott is much more concerned with pointing out that philosophical thinking has been nothing less than instrumental to the creation of our modern world.

And that story, he tells us, begins with the German logician Gottlob Frege in the latter part of the 19th century.

> "Frege took the notion of a function from mathematics, generalized it, and used that idea in logic. This led to a great deal of power, and it also led to a certain kind of general interest in functions. One of the things you can do is write a proof procedure, which can be re-expressed in terms of function-argument terminology. You can basically say that you have an effective, positive test for logical truth.
>
> "This led to this idea that there is a certain class of computable functions, and that there are both computable and non-computable functions. This revolutionized our world.
>
> "The greatest follower of Frege was Alonzo Church. He was an American mathematician at Princeton, and he was also a philosopher of mathematics. He studied a number of things, including computable functions.
>
> "Church had a student named Alan Turing, who developed a very intuitive, simple technique called a Turing machine. It wasn't really a machine. It's a mathematical framework that could compute any computable function in terms of a set of instructions on an imaginary machine, which has a finite number of states and is capable of making a distinction between zero and one.
>
> "And that took us directly to the digital age. Every computable function can be computed by a Turing machine. The key thing is that you have to make distinctions between what zero and one could be. It could be an electrical circuit being closed or an electrical circuit being open.
>
> "So anything that you could use a Turing machine for, you could, in principle, compute, using a complex, electrical circuit. This is the basis for computers, the Internet, and just about everything we use in our modern age."

Impressive though that is, the prospects for future philosophical impact might be equally tantalizing. Scott's particular research focus is on the philosophy of language, where he sees direct applications and implications of his research ranging from linguistics to the courtroom. But, ever the analytical fellow, he also recognizes that these arguments apply even more generally still to our contemporary world.

> *"Every science that breaks off from philosophy and makes enough progress so that it can become solid and non-controversial in a core domain always reaches a frontier. It's trying to advance, and it doesn't quite know how to conceptualize what to do. That is what philosophers do. That's our job: to go out to the edge of some domain that may be partially—but not completely—understood, and see what might come next—what we should be thinking about, what are the alternatives, what concepts we can employ."*

Never one to shy away from getting his philosophical hands dirty, Scott has enthusiastically plunged into the societal fray in his capacity as Director of USC's School of Philosophy.

> *"We started a new joint program in Philosophy, Politics and Law about five or six years ago. This is very unusual; and yet, it shouldn't be. It is just one example of how philosophy can connect in meaningful ways to other disciplines to advance the interests and values of those disciplines themselves, but also the direct interests of undergraduates. It's become enormously popular at a time when humanities majors are dwindling everywhere.*

> *"I also believe that making connections to philosophy can be extended to other parts of the university. This is the kind of thing that philosophy should be built to do. A discipline that goes back millennia, whose reach was in all aspects of intellectual life, should be continually striving to make these connections and to make contributions that are both philosophically interesting and interesting to people who have a different take on things."*

Not too long ago, most students found themselves faced with an unpalatable choice of either withdrawing to a monastic life of the mind or sacrificing personal growth to best impact the "real world".

But that, modern philosophers tell us, is quite simply a false dichotomy. Yet another thing we owe them.

The Conversation

I. An Analytical Introduction
From sociological musings to Gottlob Frege

HB: I took some courses in philosophy when I was younger. And at the time I distinctly remember picking up this strong bias that North American and British philosophers were the ones who engaged in logical and rigorous approaches, as opposed to those flaky, old-fashioned continentals who talked about all this metaphysical stuff and haven't fully appreciated the need for logical rigour.

Maybe that was just me, but that was certainly what I was sensing at the time—that the proper way to do things was to roll up one's sleeves and be analytical and rigorous.

SS: Well, metaphysics used to have a very bad odour at a certain stage of analytic philosophy, roughly up until 1950. Since then metaphysics has taken off.

I was a colleague of David Lewis who was considered one of the leading metaphysicians of the last half of the 20th century. There are a number of people he influenced, and there are many others who are pursuing metaphysics. It's a burgeoning enterprise.

In my mind, there is no question about whether metaphysics is a legitimate philosophical subject in which we can make progress and come to understand some things. What are the fundamental aspects of reality? What are the most fundamental parts of the universe as we know it? How far can you go in examining that question without simultaneously being a philosopher of physics? There is certainly an important strain in contemporary analytic metaphysics that says, *You better be pretty well connected with the most basic empirical science of reality in order to try and make sense of it and fit it into what you think might be a larger picture.*

That's not universally acknowledged, but it's very widely acknowledged.

HB: Is that point of view growing in popularity?

SS: Yes, it's definitely growing.

HB: Because from a physicist's perspective there is often a sense of frustration with these sorts of things. Perhaps you're a cosmologist and you're trying to understand the origins of the universe—you're looking at very large scale, law-like regularities of the universe and how they evolved, say, and you go to a party and meet a philosopher of science who claims to be looking at fundamental questions about space and time, and you think to yourself, *Well, that's what **I'm** doing. That's **my** day job. What are **you** actually doing that's any different?*

SS: My inclination is to favour the idea that philosophers have something to contribute, but only if they know the empirical science of the matter and can raise questions that the people doing the science can at least appreciate.

They may not be able to entirely pursue those questions themselves. A certain amount of quantum mechanics, for example, is about generating the right set of usable predictions about stuff. And they're pretty good at that.

But to figure out what the foundations really are and how they relate to other things in physics—these things are still up in the air. You've got to get some of the scientists to think about those things, and you've got to get some of the philosophers to think about what the science is. You've got to put those two things together. And contemporary philosophy of physics, with an orientation towards metaphysics, has a role to play there.

HB: So if analytic philosophers do metaphysics, how can they distinguish themselves from philosophers as a whole?

SS: They don't.

HB: Does that categorization have any meaning anymore?

SS: No, it doesn't. There isn't some doctrinaire view—there were at earlier stages of analytic philosophy—about what philosophy must be which eliminated whole domains of previous thought. That's not true anymore.

Most analytic philosophers today think that those restrictive doctrines were themselves the product of doctrines that were flawed, and now they have a considerably more open and almost experimental approach.

The idea is that we're not separate from other intellectual disciplines. All we demand is that you pursue whatever you're pursuing with rigour, that you articulate some criteria that can be, at least to some degree, tested—not to necessarily definitively determine who's correct, but at least provide evidence about who's correct—and that you can be well understood: you can formulate the theses and generate results that can then be taken to other domains of intellectual life to see if they contribute anything.

HB: That sounds very tolerant and open-minded.

SS: That's what we are.

HB: So I'm led to believe. But are there any members of your profession who still cling to the old divisions? Are there people who say, "*I'm not one of those analytic guys. I'm **this** or I'm **that**"*? Do those old divisions hold any meaning for people who define themselves in opposition to what analytic philosophers are or do?

SS: That's a difficult question to answer. When I started my first job at Yale in 1976, the Yale department saw itself as divided between the analytic philosophers—who were in the minority—and the others, who called themselves the pluralists. What it meant to be a pluralist, was to be anything *but* an analytic philosopher. What it was, in their minds, to be an analytic philosopher was to subscribe to some contemporary version of Carnapian logical positivism.

But by the time I started in 1976, there *weren't* any of those people around anymore. But there was still, at that time, a sense that there was some sort of divide, and that people couldn't talk across the divide.

In 1980, when I moved to Princeton, there wasn't that sort of feeling, although I should say that it's a heavily analytic department. Over the two and a half decades that I was there, there were some disputes about the role of the history of philosophy in the pursuit of contemporary philosophy. There were a few members of the department who said, "*Look, PhD students in physics, chemistry and biology are not studying the scientists of 300, 200, 100 or, even 50 years ago, so why should we do that in philosophy?*"

One particular professor said that he thought the rule ought to be that anything that's older than ten years in philosophy is the history of philosophy, and that the history of philosophy was not philosophy. We had some historians of philosophy, who were, for the most part, extremely good, disciplined historians who were also philosophically-minded.

There may still be some sense that we don't understand the relationship between contemporary, systematic philosophy and the history of philosophy very well. In my own specialized area, the philosophy of language, I don't go back very far historically. I go back to Frege from 1879 or so. I go back to Bertrand Russell, early Russell, and a bit back to Wittgenstein's *Tractatus*—although I treat that, personally, more as a historical document than something that can contribute deeply to what's going on today.

But I believe that we can not only find a terrific story of how our contemporary projects got started, but also how ideas that Frege and Russell incompletely developed can be used to solve some of the problems we face today, thereby taking their original project much further.

HB: Let me ask you to back up and tell us a little bit about that story and some of these ideas that they developed, right up until aspects of your research and what some of the contemporary issues and problems are.

I imagine that there will be a lot of people reading this who might have at least a superficial understanding of some of these ideas. They might have heard of logical positivism or the Vienna Circle. They might have heard of Wittgenstein—everybody seems to have heard of Wittgenstein, but few people seem to have actually read him carefully—myself included, I must admit.

SS: He is rather hard to read.

HB: He certainly was for me. At any rate, let's start at the beginning. What are we really talking about here?

As you mentioned earlier, Aristotle talked about notions of logic and syllogism, just as he talked about ethics, and physics, and a wide range of other things. There are those who might have heard of the *Principia Mathematica* and Russell's attempts to rigorously ground all of mathematics.

Some people may know nothing about these concepts and others may have some rough, perhaps even erroneous, notions. Perhaps you can just sketch the history of some of these core ideas that led to your current work.

SS: This is a large set of issues, a large topic, so let me begin by saying that, as I start going through this, if you feel that I am leaving something out that the reader might need to know about, just interrupt and get me to clarify things.

The story of analytic philosophy, in my opinion, really starts in 1879 with a German philosopher named Gottlob Frege. We call him a philosopher, though he was actually in the mathematics department—he was trained in mathematics—and his interest in philosophy began as an interest in the philosophy of mathematics. What is "the philosophy of mathematics"? Well, he wanted to know what the basic, mathematical objects are and how the different aspects of the study of mathematics were connected to each other and to non-mathematics.

To put it very simply, he wanted to know, *What are numbers and what is the nature of mathematical knowledge?* He came up with answers to both of those questions, which proved to be very influential in the development of logic, mathematics, and philosophy in general.

Let me just say, basically, what his answers to those questions were. *What are numbers?* Well, let's start with the number zero. Zero is the set of concepts that aren't true of anything. So, for example, the concept "not being identical with itself" is not true of anything; therefore, it's a member of the number zero.

The number one—let me give an example of one of the concepts that is a member of the number one. The concept *"having a filmed conversation with you today in the Hoose Library of Philosophy at USC"* is a concept that applies to me and only to me—and that makes it a member of the number one, which is the set of concepts of which the following is true: they're true of some x and only x.

The number two is the set of concepts true of some x and some y, where x is not identical with y, and true of nothing else. Notice that I haven't used one or two or anything like that in the definitions.

HB: Well, you can't. You're defining those concepts.

SS: That's right. So now we get some sense of what these numbers might be. What is the *successor* of a number? We'd better have the notion of a successor of a number. Well, if you have a number n, the successor of n is the set of concepts f that are true of at least one object x, such that the concept "being in f, but not identical with x" is a member of n.

What's that going to give you if you already have, say, the concept "two"? Then you've got to say, *"What is the successor of two? There has to be some concept f and something that it's true of, such that, if you kick that thing out, you'll have two."* So that will be the concept of three things, and so on. We can define all the numbers without using any numerical talk, which is essential. That's what we're doing.

Then what we do is define what a Natural number is. You might think, *"Well, a Natural number, that's pretty simple. It's just a number that you can reach by starting at zero and applying successor finitely many times.*" But then you ask yourself, "*What did I mean by "finitely many times" exactly?*" Well, by "finitely many" I mean some Natural number, n. So you can't do it *that* way, because if you do that you are including the very thing in the definition of what you're trying to define.

So what Frege ended up doing was saying something like this: "*A Natural number is a member of the smallest set that contains zero and is closed under successor.*" That is, if you start with something in the set, and you apply successor, you're still in the set. Being the smallest just means that it's a member of every set of which those conditions hold.

So now that we've got that straight, we can define counting in terms of successors, addition in terms of repeated counting, multiplication in terms of repeated addition, and so forth—thereby building up all of arithmetic. And what did we build it up from? These definitions plus what? Just ordinary, logical reasoning.

So the idea is that, if you can formalize logic and address the question *What is ordinary, logical reasoning?*—get a set of axioms and add these definitions, you end up with arithmetic, the theory of the Natural numbers.

Now, once you have arithmetic, you can define other parts of mathematics in terms of constructions on arithmetic. It's the same approach: you're always taking a higher theory, finding out what its basic, primitive vocabulary is, defining it in terms of the primitive vocabulary of the lower theory, using the axioms of the lower theory to prove the axioms of the higher theory—and now you've reduced the higher to the lower.

For Frege, the idea was to reduce all of mathematics to logic—except for geometry, he had a special thought about geometry.

HB: What was that? What was the special thought about geometry?

SS: Well, it's not something we brag about when we talk about Frege.

HB: Sure. Because it's the part that doesn't fit, presumably.

SS: Yes, well, there were already non-Euclidean geometries that were under consideration at that time...

HB: Sure. You said 1879, right? Lobachevsky had already done his thing by then, and Riemann was certainly kicking around by then as well.

SS: Yes. But Frege thought that those were purely abstract interests. What is geometry? Geometry is the study of space as we experience it.

HB: So, a form of empirical space, then?

SS: You would think so, yes. Then you would think, *If physics turned out to **require** a non-Euclidean geometry, then **that** would be the space he was talking about.*

HB: Which it does, as it happens.

SS: Right, but he didn't think that. He thought that space was a Kantian category: it was something that was contributed by our minds and our minds were built in such a way that the only way we could even conceive of space was determined by the category that our mind imposed on it, and that was Euclidean.

HB: So he was a strict Kantian in that respect.

SS: He was a strict Kantian in that respect, yes. And that's where he was lagging. But with those other aspects, he was pushing forwards.

Questions for Discussion:

*1. Do you agree with the claim that "**Anything in philosophy that's older than ten years should be regarded as the history of philosophy and not philosophy**"? Is philosophy in any way intrinsically different from physics or chemistry when it comes to appreciating past ideas?*

*2. How is the concept that "all of mathematics can be **reduced** to logic" different than the idea that "all of mathematics is **dependent** on logic"?*

3. Are you surprised at the notion of a philosopher being a member of the mathematics faculty? Do you think that such a situation could happen today?

II. Investigating Logic
The benefits of rigorous inquiry

HB: The notion seems to be that we can underpin or undergird mathematics with this logical structure. So logic, in and of itself, I guess you could say, is essential to, is the underpinning of mathematics.

SS: It's stronger than that: mathematics *is* logic in this view. Mathematical knowledge *is* logical knowledge.

There is a fundamental question here that we've just been taking for granted as if we understood what it meant—*What is logic?*

At the time that Frege invented this modern symbolic logic, the previous logic was mostly derived from Aristotle and a few other more recent people, but there was no system of logic in existence that was capable of formalizing all the reasoning in mathematics. So Frege had to invent this. And this invention turned out to be one of the great achievements of the last 150 years. Let me try to give you a very simple explanation.

With Aristotle, of course, we have syllogisms like: All As are Bs, Socrates is an A, therefore, Socrates is a B; or All As are Bs, Some Bs are Cs, therefore, some As are Cs.

Everything had to be fit into that syllogistic form. But a great many things are richer than that. There's an infinite number of valid inference forms. What you want is a language capable of expressing them, and rules that formulate when the inferences are valid.

Let's start with language. For example, think about names, like names of people, places, and things. And suppose we have predicates like "being a philosopher" and relations like "being older than", "being taller than", "being north of", "being south of", and so on. We can have relations of any number of things: two-place relations, three-place relations, four-place relations, any number.

So what are the sentences? You just start with an n-place relation and n names, and then, if you want to make complex sentences—you've got a bunch of these simple ones that you've already made that we call atomic sentences—you can conjoin them with "and", "or", "not", "if then", and "if and only if".

So *now* you have the idea of a sentence. It could be one of the simple ones or one of the more compound ones. Take one or more names out and put in what we call variables. Variables are just free-standing, singular terms to which you can assign any object as referent—"x" is an example which we're all familiar with from normal algebra.

Now you want to say, "all x" or "some x" or "at least one x" or something like that, so you just put that in front of one of these formulas. Now, what does that say? It says, *This formula is true of all objects, some objects, at least one object and so on*. That's the core.

HB: And that changes everything.

SS: That changes everything. We can now express everything that we need to express in mathematics. We can formalize all the proofs. We can write rules telling us when the inferences are guaranteed to preserve truth. Frege did this.

HB: So allow me to interject with my "man on the street" view at this point. I can imagine someone saying something like, "*It's very interesting Professor Soames, that there was this German guy in the 19th century who came up with a deeper understanding of how we ground our mathematical knowledge. It seems that it's fundamentally related to logic—or, as you say in a stronger way, effectively **is** logic. And what is this logic? It's this interesting, predicate-based system that involves quantifiers like 'some' and 'all', and all these other things that transcend what Aristotle had done. That's all well and good, but I don't really care that much about mathematics. If I'm not a mathematician, what does it mean for me?*"

A few moments ago, we were talking about the breadth of philosophical activity and how it is, to some extent, a continuum, how people are doing all sorts of other things. So perhaps another way of putting this concern is something like, *Is this type of logical framework only related to mathematics?*

SS: So, in addition to developing these formal systems, this formal language with these rules, Frege needed to say, *"Well, this is a language. How are we to understand its sentences? What are the ideas that we need in order to understand this particular language that I am using for this particular purpose?"*

I'll tell you a little bit about that—that's what turned out to have a lot of ramifications. The basic idea is that Frege took the notion of a function from mathematics, generalized it, and used that idea in logic. So, predicates and relations stand for functions, which assign their arguments of truth or falsity. You have complex formulas and we can compute what function they must stand for from the functions that the parts stand for. The quantifiers make claims about the functions: they say the functions have certain properties.

This led to a great deal of power, and it also led to a certain kind of general interest in functions. One of the things you can do is write a proof procedure: you can guarantee that, when the premises bear a certain relation to the conclusion, then if the premises are true, the conclusion is true.

You can re-express that in terms of function-argument terminology, and you can basically say that you have an effective, positive test for logical truth which is encoded in a function which, when you give it any argument and say, *"Is this a proof? Does the truth of this guarantee the truth of that?"*—if it **does** guarantee the truth of that, then the function will **always** tell you that it does, and it will **never** tell you something false.

This led to this idea that there is a certain class of computable functions, and that there are both computable and non-computable functions. This was a very interesting difference.

HB: And once something is computable, you start thinking of a decision procedure, in terms of how to actually go ahead and compute it.

SS: Exactly. That's how you get to it.

HB: You can see how this has transformed our world. Everything around us—Turing's work, computers, and so forth.

SS: Absolutely: this revolutionized our world. The greatest follower of Frege was Alonzo Church. He was an American mathematician who taught mathematics at Princeton, and he was also a philosopher of mathematics. He was the editor of the *Journal of Symbolic Logic*. He studied a number of things, including computable functions.

He had a student named Alan Turing, and Turing developed a very intuitive, simple technique called a Turing machine. It wasn't really a machine. It's a mathematical framework that could compute any computable function in terms of a set of instructions on an imaginary machine that has a finite number of states and is capable of making one distinction between zero and one.

And that's where we conceptually enter the digital age: every computable function can be computed by a Turing machine. The key thing is that you have to make distinctions between what zero and one could be. It could be an electrical circuit being closed or an electrical circuit being open.

So anything that you could use a Turing machine for, you could, in principle, compute using a complex, electrical circuit. This was the basis for all these things—computers, the Internet, and just about everything that makes up our modern world.

Questions for Discussion:

1. Why does Scott specifically talk about "the digital age" when referring to work that occurred in the 1930s? To what extent were Turing's ideas conceptually distinct from those that were used to develop technological devices such as gramophones?

2. Would it have been possible for modern computers to have been developed without the work of Frege and his followers?

3. Is there a difference between the statement "mathematics is logic" and "mathematical knowledge is logical knowledge"?

III. Language and Meaning
Minds as gateways to information

SS: That's one vital aspect of the general relevance of this work, but there's also a second. The second aspect of relevance focuses on questions like, *How can we develop a science of language? What **is** language after all?*

There are many aspects of language. Languages have a sound system. Some of them are written.

There's the *syntax* of language, which is what Noam Chomsky was so interested in, and continues to be interested in. Think of it this way: if you had a dictionary of all the words—forget about their meanings for now—which strings of words would count as sentences of language, and which would count as garbage? You need a set of principles for categorizing things and forming hierarchical relationships and developing transformational rules and so on: that's syntax.

What is *meaning*? What is it to understand a language, and what do we mean when we talk about a language? I don't think we fully know the answer to that question today, even in outline, but we got our start with Frege and Russell.

HB: How did that happen, exactly?

SS: I think it can be reconstructed this way: go back to a simple, logical language that they had a particular use for. They wanted to use the language to talk about concepts, numbers, mostly mathematical things. It didn't *have* to be mathematics, it just happened to be.

Here's the basic insight: sentences are used to talk about things—that's the central, semantic fact that you have to understand about any sentence. You have to ask, "*What is that sentence used to talk about?*" and "**What** does it say about it?" If you understand that, you've gone a long way towards understanding what it means.

How do we want to construct a theory of meaning for a language? We want to start with what the individual words stand for. We want to say how the individual words can be combined into simple sentences.

For example, the word "H" names you; another word, say, "S", stands for me; and "interview" stands for a way that two people can interact, a way a certain pair can be.

What way is that? Well, this guy can be asking questions of this guy who can be answering them. That's how we understand the parts, and when you put them together, we're saying, "*This part is interviewing that part*" and you understand. What is it for that sentence to be true? Well, it's for those two to be related in the way that "interview" says its arguments are related.

HB: It seems to me that a really groundbreaking aspect is this notion of making an equivalence between truth and meaning, so that we're looking at how to isolate the meaning of these things.

You talked about the logical framework and what it led to in terms of Alonzo Church and Turing and changing our world and so forth. But when it comes to language, when we're looking at different models, my sense is that you've got this model structure and certain things can be true within this model. But if we can say that a statement is true, then we're somehow saying something about the meaning of that. Is that a fair comment?

SS: That has been a guiding idea, starting with Frege and Russell and moving into the present day, but that idea has taken different forms and it can be developed in different ways. It may not be the whole story about meaning, but it is the core of what we learned from this approach.

The basic thought is that we can have a language that has finitely many expressions. We can specify the rules that allow infinitely many sentences. And then we can specify the conditions for each sentence that have to be satisfied by the world if that sentence is to be true.

We can do that in a compact, finite way by understanding what the parts stand for and understanding how putting them together yields a claim of a certain sort. This is called model theory, or model theoretic semantics. It was developed for these logical languages that Frege developed and Russell pursued. Tarski ended up advancing this.

The germ of the idea is that, if we understand the truth conditions of a sentence—what it is saying about the world and what way the world has to be in order for it to be true—then we have the beginnings of a theory of meaning for language. A key, related question is, *How do we make that robust enough to give us everything we're going to need in a theory of meaning?*

HB: You say, *"What does it say about the world?"* I'm guessing that this is where this notion of possible worlds comes from, because one can imagine that there are worlds where this is not true, where this doesn't apply. So we're looking at possible environments, possible worlds, possible models, and possible conditions whereby this property, whatever it is, is actually true.

We're getting closer, I think, to the point where there's a problem, where these ideas start to break down. This is where I want to get to for the next stage of our discussion. So far, everything we've spoken about has been, more or less, a raging success story, it seems to me.

Frege comes along and he says, *"I'm interested in the foundations of mathematics. Mathematics is equivalent to logic. Here's what I mean by logic."* After a bunch more work, model-building, creating proofs, and turning cranks, that leads to the development of computer science which leads to all sorts of other wonderful things that have changed our world.

Then people look at these ideas from within a philosophy of language perspective, making an equivalence between the truth of statements and their meanings in different models and in different possible worlds. Everything seems rosy in that story.

But let me just back up for a moment and refer to Russell, where he talks about the relationship of philosophy to science. He says words to the effect of, *"Philosophy is what we don't know and as soon as we know something, then it becomes science."* There's this sense of philosophy giving birth to science, where philosophers are portrayed as essentially sitting around in the desert asking, *"What's up there?"*— and, eventually, through their efforts, people start treating these ideas more rigorously, and then, once it becomes sufficiently rigorous, suddenly you get physics, say.

That's a very crude synopsis of the process, but my understanding is that the idea is that philosophers are asking these basic, fundamental, questions and then as soon as we start having some very clear, distinct pathway towards developing concrete solutions, it becomes a science.

In one of your recent essays, you talk about how, under this model structure you've described, with meaning being equivalent to truth within these models, that one might think, *Well, that's it then. Linguistics can take over, we can turn a crank, and we can start understanding everything there is about meaning. The philosophers can then get out of the way, according to Russell, and move on to other things.* But it turns out that that's not the case, right?

SS: Well, there is a lot of very good crank-turning that continues to go on and there is a lot of progress that is still to be made in that general line. But there are a number of things that are left out. The biggest thing that's left out is the second half of the equation, as you might put it.

What is meaning? Well, we've said that these sentences impose conditions that the world must satisfy if they are to be true. And so meaning must just be the truth conditions that a sentence imposes on the world.

The other side of the coin is that language is not just something that is about things in the world. Language is used by *agents*, and it's the agents using the language in a certain way that leads to the fact that the sentence has the meaning and carries the information that it does. That, ultimately, is what explains the truth conditions of the sentence. Moreover, the cognitive relation that the agent bears to the sentence is something that imposes conditions—certain meanings impose conditions on those who entertain them, just as they impose truth conditions on the world that they represent.

Russell and Frege weren't so interested in coming up with a science of language that had both sides of this story covered. They were interested in using a powerful enough language to solve the philosophical problems that they were interested in. But if we are to have a science of language, we must understand both sides of this equation, which we don't yet.

HB: You emphasize this notion of a cognitive act: when we exchange information, there is a "we" who is exchanging information.

SS: We *think* there is an agent doing the thinking, and how that thinking is done has important connections with what the information actually is.

HB: And that itself contains information. It is a form of meta-information.

SS: Yes. Up until now, we have not had a model of information that makes that a part of it. What has the model of information been? Very simply put—we'll go back to the possible worlds idea—here's what you can do and here's what lots of people do today, very effectively and well.

They take a language—it used to be these formal, logical languages, but now this is applied to natural languages or fragments of natural languages—and they say, "*I will show you how to assign contents to the individual words and phrases and how to interpret the manners of construction that will allow you to derive a theorem of the following kind for every one of the many sentences in this fragment.*"

And the theorem will be—I'm going to use a little terminology that I'll have to explain shortly—*S is true at a possible world W, if and only if, at that possible world W so and so.*

That "so and so" gives the conditions the world must satisfy in order for that sentence, as it's used with this meaning, to be true.

We are very good at that.

And if you say, "*Okay, fine. What, then, is the **information** contained by that sentence S?*" Well, clearly it's the set of possible worlds in which the thing is true. That's what the information is. Information is, *What do you know when you know that S is true*? Well, you know the actual world is one of these particular possible worlds. That's the basic story.

Now, what are some of the problems that we run into when we follow this model?

One of the problems is that sentences true in the same possible worlds express the same proposition. That means that every necessary truth—well, there's really only one. There are many sentences that happen to express the one, necessary truth, but one implication of this representation is that, say, I wouldn't be able to know that 1 = 1 without knowing every fact of mathematics, all of which are necessary.

That's a fundamental problem: it gives us a conception of representation, which is too coarse-grained. So there must be more to truth conditions than there is to sets of possible worlds in which they are true.

When I was talking informally about truth conditions, what did I say? I said, *Well, what is it to know the **meaning** of a sentence*? It's to know that it's talking about *this particular thing* and, it's saying of it that it's *this particular way*; and then, what's truth going to mean? Well, it's going to be true in the case that that thing **really is** that way.

HB: You give a very concrete example in one of your essays. You examine the question, "What is a proposition?"

SS: Yes. A proposition: a piece of information.

What is a piece of information? It's something that we can use a sentence to express. We know that. What do we *do* with sentences? Sometimes we assert things. What are we asserting when we use two sentences that express the same piece of information? We're asserting that information.

Information can be something asserted, something believed, the contents of some sentences. What is it that can play that role?

The first thing you have to ask is, *How tied to language must this be?* It is tied. We use sentences to express information, but we can believe things, animals can believe things, and merely possible agents can believe things, without using the English sentence that we use, and sometimes without using any sentence at all.

A piece of information—what must it do? Perhaps it must do many things, but one thing it must do is represent something as being some way. Then we know what truth is going to be—that piece of information is going to be true *if there is such a thing and it is that way*. What kind of thing can it be that we bear this relation to: we can believe it, we can assert it, we can doubt it, but it's something that can be true or false depending on what it represents and whether the thing is that way.

Now, one thing it *can't* be is a set of possible worlds, because what does it represent? What does a set with, say, three worlds in it represent?

HB: Nothing in particular.

SS: Right. It doesn't necessarily represent anything. Even if you were to play a game and assign truth conditions to those sets of worlds, we've seen that there are many different propositions that you'd assign the same set of worlds to. But they wouldn't mean the same thing. They wouldn't be what you believe, or what you assert. So we know it can't be those things.

What can it be? Russell and Frege thought that there *was* such a thing. They knew that sentences were, somehow, used to express them, but they couldn't figure out what it was, and they ended up giving up on the idea.

At that point, much of the tradition turned to sentences and truth conditions, which then got augmented to truth relative to a possible world state, and then propositions came back again—as sets of possible worlds—and then we arrived at the problem that we're talking about right now. That's where we find ourselves today.

We need the notion of something which isn't *itself* a piece of language, which represents things as being a certain way and so can be true or false and have truth conditions. Where are we going to get this notion of a representational thing? My belief is that we start with the fundamental presupposition that it's *minds* that represent. Minds are the representational entities.

Minds, when they represent things in a certain way, do so by following certain cognitive processes. Let me just give a name—and that's all it is—when I look at this table and I see it as brown, my visual system represents this thing as brown; it, so to speak, predicates being brown of that thing that I'm in visual contact with.

HB: So that's a logical antecedent to the idea of—

SS: Yes. That is the antecedent to language, but it's a *piece of information*. Moreover, I can form a perceptual *belief* that it's brown. If I have the concept of a table, I can form the belief that it's a brown table. All of these things I can do. I can do some of them whether I have any language or not, and as we get more complicated, I can do it with some given language, but it doesn't matter which language I happen to speak.

HB: Is it that you *can* do it or is it more that you *must* do it, in terms of that being an essential aspect of what we previously called a proposition?

SS: Let me put it this way: I can predicate brownness of this table simply visually without using any language, or I can close my eyes and say, "*This table is brown*," and I'm using the language to perform the same predication. The two are both acts in which I predicate something of an object, but they differ in terms of how I'm performing that act: in one case I'm using language to do it, in the other case, my visual system is doing it for me.

Let's take a piece of information to be one of these acts predicating brownness of this thing. Then let's look at the different forms that act can take: using language, using perception, using one's imagination. Those are all propositions as well. They're slightly different cognitive acts, but they have the same representational content because they're all predications of brownness of that object. They have identical truth conditions. They impose the same conditions on the world.

They impose different conditions on the agent who's performing the action: one requires some language, another requires visual perception, another requires imagination. We start from there, the idea that there are two sides. There is this mental operation that I can perform, that any animal with a visual system that can represent colours can perform. Maybe their neurology is different from mine, but somehow their neurology is accomplishing this and my neurology is accomplishing it as well.

Questions for Discussion:

1. By asserting the concept of "mind" as the fundamental representational entity, to what extent does Scott extend the domain of his framework to encompass neuroscience and cognitive science more generally? Is it logically conceivable that one day a neuroscientist might be able to objectively determine the extent to which someone "possesses a piece of information"?

2. Might it be argued that I need to have a comprehensive theory of consciousness before I can start formally invoking the concept of "mind"?

3. How might Scott's ideas about how to value "a piece of information" be related to mathematical treatments of "information theory" or a quantum information theorist's views that "all information is inherently physical"?

4. In what ways are the concepts discussed in this chapter related to the notion of "abstractness"? If I maintain that two theories are at some level fundamentally equivalent, say, then how, exactly, have I generated the notion of "equivalence" on which such a "piece of information" depends?

IV. Legal Applications
Some concrete examples

HB: This is a hard sort of conversation to have in real time, and I'm very impressed by your ability to pull it off. But I'm guessing that many people who are reading through it are finding aspects of it pretty tough going.

So I think it's time for some examples—let's move from the abstract to the more concrete and talk about some specific implications of these ideas.

SS: I'll talk a little bit about the kinds of implications that I think the philosophy of language can have for one specific aspect of the philosophy of law, what you might call the philosophy of legal interpretation.

What does an interpreter do and how should we understand that? By an interpreter, I mean somebody who takes a law that has been promulgated by a legislative authority—it's already been passed. You may be working for an administrative agency and have to come up with what they'll call rules for implementing the law. You may be a judge who is called upon to render a verdict in some case in which there's a dispute about whether the law applies and what it means.

There's a question about how we should think about that process. The process begins with what one might call the "content" of the law. There's usually a written text, and that written text, as we say, encodes or expresses some content or information. So the question is, *What does that written text require? What falls under it and what doesn't?*

The first task of a legal interpreter is to discover what that representational content is. You might think, *Well, the words are there, so it's easy: you just read them and understand what they're saying.*

That would be true if the context in which those words were used by the legislative body or authority made no contribution whatsoever to the information that was being asserted or stipulated by the body in question.

But that's *not* true if we look at ordinary uses of language. It's not true that context plays no role in determining the content of what words are used to assert, or to stipulate, or to order. If you look closely at what goes on when judges are looking at some of these legal texts, it's not always true in the law either. The context *does* sometimes provide information which is not present in the words that are used.

There was one particular case that I'll mention that provides a clear way to grasp this. It's a famous case everybody talks about, the Smith case, about a provision that was passed by Congress which stipulated that, if you committed a felony and you did it using a gun, you would have an extra five years attached to your sentence. The actual wording was "using or carrying a gun", but for our purposes we'll say "using".

Well, what is "using a gun", exactly? If somebody said to you, "*Have you ever used a gun?*" In most contexts, people would think they were being asked, "*Have you ever used a gun as a weapon?*"

Even if, for example, you inherited an old rifle from your grandfather as part of his estate and you sold it and made a profit, and then some body were to ask you if you had "used a gun", you probably wouldn't think, *Well, I used it then*, because you would likely still interpret "using a gun" as "using it as a weapon". So, even though the question doesn't explicitly say, "as a weapon", often, the context indicates that that's what was at stake.

And this case came to the Supreme Court. The fellow, Smith, had a gun, but he was trading it for drugs. The question was, "*Should he have an extra five years added on to his sentence because he used the gun in a drug trafficking crime?*"

The court ruled that he **should have** the extra five years tacked on because the plain meaning of "used a gun", in English, is "using a gun as a weapon, a paperweight, or for some other purpose".

The thinking was that Congress naturally *could have been* more specific, but since they weren't, we must take the plain meaning at its face value, and the plain meaning is simply "to use a gun". Period.

That happened because they were looking at the *meanings* of the words instead of the *intentionality*—instead of what the words were used to assert or stipulate. So the first thing we must do is find out what was asserted or stipulated.

HB: And distinguish between these two, presumably.

SS: Yes, that's right. Now, suppose you're an interpreter and you've done that. You still have a hard case in front of you. Why? Well, perhaps the language says, *No vehicles in the park*. Well, **what's** a vehicle? We know cars are vehicles, and motorcycles are vehicles, and trucks are vehicles, but are *skateboards? Wheelchairs? Tricycles?* Are little red wagons vehicles? Well, it's vague, isn't it?

When a concept is vague, it doesn't clearly fall under what was asserted, nor is it completely clear that it's excluded by what's asserted. It's simply left open—the law is silent about that question. Nevertheless, you have a case in front of you, so you have to do *something*. In many cases it will be highly impractical to go back to the town council and ask, "*What exactly did you mean?*"

So you need some principle.

Well, what would we do in an ordinary situation—when it wasn't a legal matter—if you told me that we were going to meet up at a certain point, but it's vague exactly where and when? I would try to discern what we were going to do when we met. Perhaps we were going to meet for lunch and we had narrowed it down to, at least, a block area, but there was only one restaurant in that area. Then I would go to that place and think, *Well, I should interpret him as having directed me to go there*.

So in a legal context, we look at **why** the law was passed. What was the rationale? What were they trying to accomplish? Were they trying to eliminate noise and pollution, so they were thinking specifically about motor vehicles? Did they have some other motivation in mind?

Once you come up with what the rationale was and you say, "*Well, it's silent about this case,*" you make the minimum modification in the law that best advances the rationale for the original law and apply it to this particular case; and, if that becomes a precedent, the law has changed to a certain degree—it has become more precise than it was before.

HB: So there's a decision procedure right there.

SS: Yes. Of course, it requires judgment because it's not a real algorithm, but it gives you criteria.

HB: Well, we're not robots. We live in the real world with all sorts of shades of grey, but at least it gives you some sense—if you're a judge or if you're on a jury—you don't just throw up your hands and say, "*Gosh, I don't know what to do.*" You have some clear sense, difficult though it may be, as to a prioritized sequence of what you should be looking for, where you should go. It gives some sense of direction.

SS: Yes. And notice that the question wasn't, "*What does the judge think the purpose of the law should have been?*" or "*What's the judge's view on what vehicles should be around?*"

No, the judge is making the decision—and it takes a certain amount of discretion on her part to do so—but what she's trying to do is advance the original rationale for the law, where the rationale is basically the values and arguments that were articulated publicly to advance the law and to explain what it was trying to achieve.

There are certain cases in which the law, which may have been passed at some other time, simply didn't envision a certain situation, but some decision must be made. And whatever decision is made will change the law in some degree.

When the court does this, the court must make new law. The idea that courts never make new law, that they never legislate, is not correct. They sometimes must do so, but they must do so in a deferential way, trying to make the minimum change that would advance the rationale—not their particular rationale, but the rationale that was offered in favour of the law in the first place. It makes sense of this core idea of our judicial system that the different branches and powers are separate and confined.

Questions for Discussion:

1. Do you agree or disagree with the court's decision about extending the sentence to the person who was convicted of trading a gun for drugs?

2. Should legislators be encouraged to phrase the wording of their laws in such a way as for others to more easily recognize its intent? Might there be times when legislators deliberately opt for being vague about the wording of the laws they are creating?

3. What do you think Scott means, exactly, when he discusses how, by encouraging courts to focus on how best to interpret the intentionality of legislators, we are "making sense of the idea that the different branches and powers are separate and confined"?

V. Changing the Culture
Philosophy everywhere

HB: Earlier, you were telling me that there is some level of structural integration between the department of philosophy and the law faculty at USC. Is this sort of structural integration happening more broadly? Is USC taking the lead on this, or is this something that is, generally, a widespread phenomenon?

SS: It's not widespread. When we started this program—Philosophy, Politics and Law—it was about five or six years ago, and we were not aware of any program like this in the United States. Since we've started it, I think I've heard of one or two similar programs, but I don't remember exactly where they are, and I'm not sure they were all philosophy, politics and law—some might have had economics instead of law, like at Oxford.

This is very unusual—and yet, it shouldn't be. This is one example of how philosophy can connect in meaningful ways to other disciplines in ways that advance the interests and values of those disciplines themselves, but also the direct interests of undergraduates. It's become enormously popular at a time when humanities majors are dwindling everywhere.

I also believe that making connections to philosophy can be extended to other parts of the university. We'd very much like to have a philosophy and physics program that would get people to combine the study of both. They would come out with both a B.A. and a Master's in it, because it requires pretty intensive training.

This is the kind of thing that philosophy should be built to do. A discipline that goes back millennia, whose reach was in all aspects of intellectual life, should be continually striving to make these connections and to make contributions that are both philosophically interesting and interesting to people who have a different take on things.

HB: An obvious point to make is that, not only does it expand the reach of philosophy and thus provide beneficial effects towards these other disciplines—law, physics, what have you—but it also replenishes philosophy itself.

The very contact with these other areas—thinking in some particular way, interaction, and interchange—enables philosophy itself to progress by being exposed to different ideas. So it's not just a case of "applying" philosophical ideas, it's this sense of replenishment on both sides.

SS: It certainly is. I gave some lectures in Germany last year on some of the material about information and language and things like that. The title of the lecture series was something like, What is the Agenda of 21st-Century Philosophy?

After there lectures there was a strain of questioning coming from some of the students and even some of the professors, especially as I was emphasizing the way in which philosophy contributes to the study of what is information, which we think is in the process of giving birth to a genuine science.

And they said, "*Yeah, but what happens when these things all become science? There won't be anything for philosophers to do anymore.*"

My first reaction to that, which I still feel the same about, was, "*Do you **seriously** think that there are fewer philosophical questions out there to be investigated now than there were in Aristotle's time? There are surely more.*"

Every science that breaks off from philosophy and makes enough progress so that it can become solid and non-controversial in a core domain always reaches a frontier.

It's trying to advance, and it doesn't quite know how to conceptualize what to do. That is what philosophers do. That's our job: to go out to the edge of some domain that may be partially, but not completely, understood, and see what might come next: what we should be thinking about, what are the alternatives, what concepts we can employ.

HB: This sounds to me like a strategy for engagement.

SS: We are doing more of it, and it will increase over time. When you talked about the fact that this is not just applied philosophy, but a replenishment of philosophy itself, another way of putting that is, *"That's what philosophy is: it's looking over the horizon and discovering how we can expand our reach, understanding what questions we can be asking."*

Yes, that takes a different form now because there's so much other knowledge available. Yes, if you're in my department and you're working on the philosophy of quantum mechanics, you and I don't have much overlap in terms of our philosophical expertise. This is how it is in philosophy: philosophy departments are full of specialized researchers. Many of these specialties are specialties in the sense that they relate philosophy to linguistics, mathematics, physics, to all sorts of things. And there will be more.

Of course, we have some specialization within what are more traditionally thought of as core, philosophical problems. But we exist in an age of specialization. Philosophers do not overcome specialization—they're specialized too—but they take a slightly broader, different perspective on law, politics, physical science, mathematics, and so forth. They raise some questions that wouldn't ordinarily be raised. They help make advances. They help expand what we do.

Questions for Discussion:

*1. Do you think that philosophy should be a mandatory course for all students at the high-school or university level? Readers interested in this topic are referred to several Ideas Roadshow conversations that touch on this issue, such as Chapter 5 of **Inflated Expectations: A Cosmological Tale** with Princeton University physicist Paul Steinhardt, Chapter 2 of **How Social Science Creates the World** with UC Berkeley political scientist Mark Bevir and Chapter 1 of **Learning and Memory** with UCLA cell biologist Alcino Silva.*

2. Are there any negative aspects to interdisciplinary programs such as philosophy and law or philosophy and physics? If so, to what extent can they be compensated for?

3. Do you think that this conversation is too Western-centric? Are there important philosophical ideas from other cultures and traditions that have been overlooked here?

VI. Gödelian Challenges

Making sense of the incompleteness theorems

HB: I'd like to return briefly to analytic philosophy, and some aspects of logic in particular. Earlier you mentioned how the glossed-over summary I gave—"we've taken care of mathematics, and now we can move on to these other fields"—isn't quite correct.

There might well be some people who are thinking to themselves, *Hang on a minute—there was this Gödel fellow with his incompleteness theorems. What does that mean in terms of logical structures that you're talking about? What sort of ramifications does that have for any of your work, be it in the philosophy of language or be it in aspects of the philosophy of mathematics?*

SS: I'm working on my second volume of the history of analytic philosophy now. I'm just coming up to the chapters on Gödel, Tarski and Church. At that point, the study of logical and formal systems became itself a domain of inquiry, and a domain of solid and surprising results. Gödel's results were among the most surprising.

HB: My understanding is that the incompleteness theorems led to this upheaval of what we know as logical systems, but there seems to be some degree of variation as to what they imply and what they really mean. Do the incompleteness theorems have any clear and obvious relevance for the philosophy of language, in your view? Or might they? And, if so, how?

SS: There are some certain hard facts that are simply proven, certain hard limitations that we run up against. Do those limitations prevent us from doing things that we'd like to do? No. How could they, possibly?

Gödel demonstrated that certain things are impossible. We don't need a decision procedure for first-order logical truths in order to use first-order sentences to communicate information. To me, what is fascinating is that all these results are really applications of paradoxes, and they are constructive applications of paradoxes.

We can show that, if certain things that you thought might be true were true, a paradox is generated and you get a contradiction, which indicates that those things can't possibly be true.

We are not at all at the end of using that form of reasoning—and indeed, the very paradoxes that provided what was really going on with the Gödel incompleteness theorem. We are still finding more implications. The liar paradox is the key paradox—for example, *"What I'm saying right now is not true"*. There are, of course, much more interesting and complicated versions of it.

HB: My sense is that, to a certain extent, things hinge on the idea of meta-structure, and that Russell's paradox was also an aspect of that, to the extent that he's looking at the sets of sets. Is that your view as well?

SS: This is a controversial matter. I don't see it that way myself. There are what are called "semantic paradoxes", but I don't think Russell's paradox is like that.

HB: So there are different types of paradoxes?

SS: I think so, although I'm not sure I understand fully what's going on.

One of the things that's interesting about the Gödel incompleteness theorem is that it's very closely related to a theorem called "the arithmetical indefinability of arithmetical truth". That's a Tarski theorem. It's really just Tarski using the Gödel methodology to develop the same thing.

In Gödel, you've got a formal language, which is arithmetic. What does arithmetic talk about? Well, it talks about numbers. But you develop a coding system so that you associate each sentence of the language with a number, and there's an effective procedure so that, given any sentence, you can figure out what its Gödel number is; and, given any number, you can figure out first whether it's the Gödel number of anything and—if it is—what it's the Gödel number of. So it's effectively decidable that the numbering system has to be that way.

What you then do is take some of the sentences and formulas of the language, which naturally talk about numbers. Then, since you've set up a coding system, you can take them as talking about expressions in the language. You can even take them as talking about themselves.

What would it be for arithmetical truth to be definable in arithmetic? That would mean the set of Gödel numbers of true sentences is the Gödel number of some formula in the language of arithmetic. That formula, if there were such a thing, could serve as the truth predicate for the language of arithmetic.

Well, you can prove that, if there *were* such a formula, then the liar paradox would be reconstructible in arithmetic, and it would either have to be true or not true. But to assume that it's true, you'll get a contradiction that it's *not* true, and to assume that it's not true, you'll get a contradiction that it *is* true. So the conclusion people draw is that there is no formula for a language of arithmetic that has those properties.

What makes it seem very puzzling is that what you have to assume about the language of arithmetic in order to prove this—and then prove it can't have its own truth predicate—is a very mild set of assumptions that are obviously satisfied by English. Or it at least looks like they are easily satisfied by English.

You find yourself saying thinks like, "*There is no truth predicate of English.*" English doesn't have its own truth predicates? That's hard to wrap one's head around. After all, there is this word "true", and there is this phrase, "*... is a true sentence of English.*" You're telling me that's not a truth predicate? It certainly *seems* like a truth predicate of English.

But if it's *not* a truth predicate, that would have to mean either that it applies to something which isn't a true sentence of English—well, that couldn't be—or there are some true sentences of English, which are such that, if you say, "*It's a true sentence of English,*" then that sentence is false. And how could that possibly be?

In some sense, it *couldn't* possibly be. So what conclusion do you draw from all of this? This strikes me as still an unresolved question. Yet it appears to be an application of a fundamental theorem: everybody regards the arithmetical indefinability of arithmetical truth—which is just a simple application of the Gödel methodology—to be a fundamental truth.

I've tried to state the assumptions and apply them to English in one of my books, and it looks pretty persuasive. Now, of course, the result *can't* be right, and there are different ways you can imagine *why* it isn't right. But what is the *real* reason the result isn't right?

This is an issue that's still deep, important, and unresolved, and we've got people working on it.

HB: Fascinating stuff. Is there anything I have omitted?

SS: I'm sure there are lots of things.

HB: Okay, so let me rephrase that question, because it wasn't terribly well-posed. This is the problem with talking to an analytic philosopher: he'll quickly let you know when you're not saying something suitably precisely.

So, let me try again: Have I omitted something particularly significant? Is there anything specific you would like to add at this point?

SS: Yes, I'd like to have two or three more of these conversations.

HB: That would be wonderful. But for the moment, anyway, I sense we should bring this one to a close. Thank you very much, Scott, for your time.

SS: You're welcome. My pleasure.

Questions for Discussion:

1. How would you describe the key results of Gödel's incompleteness theorems in your own words?

2. To what extent do you think Gödel's incompleteness theorems have influenced the development of mathematics or any other field of inquiry? How might they in the future?

Continuing the Conversation

Readers interested in a more detailed treatment of some of the topics discussed in this conversation are referred to Scott's books *The World Philosophy Made: From Plato to the Digital Age*, *The Analytic Tradition in Philosophy: A New Vision* and *The Analytic Tradition in Philosophy, Volume 1—The Founding Giants*.

Plato's Heaven

A User's Guide

A conversation with James Robert Brown

Introduction

Mathematical Metaphysics

If someone tells you that he's just discovered that the fundamental laws of physics are wrong, you'll likely be pretty sceptical. But depending on his reputation, you might be inclined to hear him out for a moment or two, curious to know what spectacular new evidence he's claimed to have found.

But if he tells you that he's stumbled upon a new proof that 7+5 no longer equals 12, I'm fairly confident that you won't even take the time to listen to him for a moment longer, no matter who he is.

Why the change in attitude?

Because mathematics is, well, *different* from science. It's not terribly difficult to imagine nature being something else again from the way it happens to be: the proton much heavier, DNA made from three essential nucleotides instead of four, the Earth millions of years younger or older. Not only *could* things conceivably be quite different from the way that they actually are, we're forever recognizing just how wrong we were. Indeed, the long march of scientific progress is little more than a series of discoveries forcing us to revise our old ways of thinking, from the causes of tides to why things burn.

Mathematics progresses too, of course. Its rapidly evolving sub-disciplines—from logic to fractals, network topology to optimization theory—have not only kept pace with physics, chemistry, biology, engineering and economics, but have fundamentally influenced the development of all of them.

Meanwhile, the pristine world of "pure mathematics", with its detached realms of number theory and multi-dimensional geometrical abstractions, plows methodically ahead, regularly opening up new research while steadily clearing up niggling old mysteries.

In 1994, after several centuries of collective mathematical frustration, Princeton mathematician Andrew Wiles managed to prove Pierre de Fermat's deceptively off-handed claim that no three positive integers a, b and c can satisfy the relation an + bn = cn for any number n greater than 2. In finally elevating this infamous 17th-century conjecture to the status of a bona fide theorem, Wiles assured himself an intense 15 minutes of global fame together with a considerably more lasting place in the mathematical Pantheon. His proof utilizes a combination of esoteric mathematical constructs such as elliptical curves, modular forms and deformations—none of which, it is pointedly worth emphasizing, existed in Fermat's day.

So mathematics clearly evolves and makes progress. And yet, when a mathematician proves a new theorem or finds important connections between two areas previously thought to be independent of each other, what is she really doing? Well, making a discovery, it seems. But then, where is the "thing", exactly, that is being discovered? Where was it *before* the discovery occurred? And how did she "see" it, exactly?

In biology, when a new virus is found, or when we develop some specific understanding of, say, how proteins are folded, we feel justifiably confident that we have uncovered something that nature had been hiding from us all along.

Mathematicians, on the other hand, who spend their time in the abstract land of algebraic topology and infinite-dimensional spaces, have no such recourse to the natural world to ground their discoveries. So *what*, exactly, are they actually doing?

Opinions vary considerably. But most people, when pushed, will concede that mathematics must be some sort of man-made activity, an elaborate form of symbol manipulation according to a set of rules that we have all come to naturally agree upon: a sophisticated, rigorously consistent, abstract game.

University of Toronto philosophy professor James Robert Brown, however, will have none of it. For Brown, our age-old intuitions are quite correct; mathematical objects are every bit as real as their physical counterparts and exist completely independent of us. In other words, mathematicians operationally behave just like any other scientist when it comes to pushing the boundaries of their discipline: any new discovery they make simply corresponds to a recognition of what is already there.

But where is *"there"*, exactly? It cannot be in space and time, because mathematical objects don't exist in the world around us—you might find a circular object on the table across from you, but you won't ever find the perfect circle or π or Fermat's Last Theorem anywhere.

No matter, maintains Brown adamantly. They have their own unique, timeless world outside of us, just like Plato told us all those years ago. Platonism might sound crazy at first to the modern ear, Jim admits, but look a bit more carefully and some of the doubts begin to fade.

In the first place, an impressive selection of the most celebrated mathematical minds in recent history were unequivocal Platonists—people like Gottlob Frege, G.H. Hardy and Kurt Gödel.

"If these smart guys believe it," he declares amiably, *"we should at least take it seriously."*

Yet there is much more to his argument than this jauntily self-acknowledged "shameless appeal to authority". There is something about mathematics, Jim reminds us, that is radically different from formal symbol manipulation according to some arbitrarily invoked rules. Mathematics, in other words, is simply not like chess.

"'5 + 7 = 12'," he declares, *"has a completely different feel from, 'Bishops move diagonally'."*

After all, it's not difficult to imagine a large spectrum of chess-like games with differently moving pieces, each internally consistent and more or less enjoyable to play strictly according to the subjective proclivities of the players. But there's simply no way to convince us that 4 + 7 = 12 is somehow just as meaningful, valid or truthful as 5 + 7 = 12 if we would just be prepared to change a few axioms. Of course, we could simply name things differently (i.e. deciding to now say "4" when we really mean "5"), but that is not at all the same thing.

Still, taking Platonism seriously is hard to do. For one thing, if there really *is* this separate world of mathematical objects existing outside of space and time, how do we, as decidedly real-world entities, ever gain access to it? Clearly, nothing described by science is going to help us, precisely because we are no longer in the domain of the natural world. So how do we make contact with this bizarre metaphysical world of mathematical entities, exactly?

Jim doesn't pretend to have a complete answer. But he has spent considerable time fleshing out the intriguing notion that in some cases, at least, pictures might play a role. By explicitly highlighting a number of visual representations that immediately provide us with that "Aha moment" of proof recognition, he goes a considerable way towards convincing even the most sceptical that some visual aids can become "windows to Plato's Heaven".

Moreover, he reminds us, however mysterious the mechanics of interacting with the Platonic world might be, when you get right down to it, the everyday interactions with physical objects are hardly straightforward either.

> *"When it comes to ordinary perception, what exactly is understood? I see a coffee cup on my table. Photons come from the cup, enter my eye, interact with the rods and cones inside; a signal is sent down the optic nerve into the visual cortex, and so on. This much—the physiological part of the process—is understood very well. But what about my sensation of the cup and my belief that there is a cup on the table? No one has the foggiest idea how these sensations and*

beliefs are formed. This is the mind-body problem—and it's utterly unsolved... How the physical process brings about our internal beliefs about the world is a very great mystery. It is just as great a mystery as how mathematical entities bring about mathematical belief. Of course, it would be wonderful to understand both, but our ignorance in the mathematical case is no worse than our ignorance in the case of everyday objects."

Such disarmingly honest statements of our wide-ranging ignorance are typical of Jim. Many academics stubbornly refrain from enunciating clear metaphysical positions, naturally opting to hedge away their personal discomfort in a sea of impenetrable jargon.

Mathematicians, meanwhile, whom one might naively expect to feel some sort of pressure to clearly articulate what it is they are actually doing all day, typically do their utmost to ignore the issue altogether. For them, Platonism is "the metaphysics that dare not speak its name": virtually all succumb to it during their working hours, but few will publicly defend it.

Not so James Robert Brown, who publicly avers his views with the same cheerful straightforwardness as he recognizes their deep unpopularity. His opponents are numerous and unrelenting: Formalists, Conventionalists, Intuitionists, Constructivists, Physicalists, Positivists, Naturalists and more. Like the general who, after being informed that the enemy has him surrounded, replies *"Excellent! Now we can attack in any direction!"*, Brown strides off confidently towards Platonism's Golden Land, armed with nothing but his intellectual convictions and genial candour. Not content with simply being a mathematical Platonist, his many years of carefully studying the role of scientific thought experiments has convinced him to extend his beliefs towards the physical sciences as well, leading him to offer up nothing less than a Platonic interpretation of quantum mechanics.

This will likely strike many as pretty far-fetched, if not downright crazy—even Jim, characteristically, admits to being "not too sanguine" about its prospects. But then, nobody ever accused quantum theory of making too much sense. Why not add a bit of Platonism to the mix?

The Conversation

I. Introducing Platonism
An explanation for what mathematics really is

HB: As you know, we're here to chat about mathematical Platonism. Maybe I shouldn't even say "mathematical Platonism"—perhaps I should just say "Platonism", because there might be other aspects associated with Platonism that you might want to talk about.

As I was saying to you earlier, sometimes when I talk to people and say, "*There is this really cool question about to what extent mathematics **really exists** and, if so, **where** it exists and how we might have access to it*," and I use the words "philosophy" or "Platonism" people—often very educated, reasonably curious people—have a tendency to recoil in horror, convinced that any subject that involves a combination of mathematics and philosophy is definitely something that should be avoided at all costs.

Which is, I think, a real shame since this topic has long struck me as one of the relatively few deeply profound and fascinating ideas that anyone can have a clear grasp of after just a few moments of reflection.

So, perhaps the thing to do is to simply dive in, with me asking you what Platonism is, exactly, before moving on to its history, strengths and weaknesses, and eventually explore your particular beliefs and insights.

So what is it? What are we talking about here, exactly? What do we mean by "Platonism"?

JB: Well, maybe the easiest way to get an entry into contemporary Platonism—never mind the actual Plato, just what we call Platonism today—is to take simple things in mathematics.

So think of all of the mathematical things that you already believe: two plus three equals five, that there are an infinitude of numbers, that there are an infinitude of prime numbers, and so on. And then ask yourself, "*Are all those facts, those mathematical facts, are they like **physics**?*"

When I say, *Protons are heavier than electrons*, I'm saying—at least I hope I'm saying—something true about the world, a statement of something that is independent of me, something that's *out there* that physicists have discovered. Is math like *that*? Or is it more like this: *Bishops move diagonally in the game of chess.*

That's also true, but it's something that we've obviously created.

HB: Because we could have made bishops move in any particular way we wanted.

JB: That's right.

So the first question is, *Which side are you on?* Now, some people opt for the game. They think, *Oh, it's an awful lot like a game.* And that will give you certainty in mathematics. I mean, it's *certain* that bishops move diagonally simply because we have agreed that they do.

HB: Sure. By definition.

JB: That's right: by definition. On the other hand, if you think that mathematics is somehow or other *out there*, waiting; that mathematicians actually make discoveries, just like physicists make discoveries about the world, then you are on the Platonic side of things: mathematics has a kind of independent existence from us.

Another way of putting it is to ask the question, *If no conscious beings existed anywhere in the universe, would it still be true that there are infinitely many prime numbers?*

HB: Right. Or two plus three equals five or—

JB: That's right, anything like that at all. Clearly, if there were no intelligent beings, then bishops wouldn't move diagonally. There'd just be no fact to the matter about it at all. It wouldn't have been created.

HB: But those of a Platonic persuasion would certainly *not* believe that two plus three equals five is simply one of a possible number of alternatives that we have opted for by definition—that somehow two plus three *could* have equally well equalled six. Or it could have equalled seventeen.

JB: That's right. The idea here is that there are basic facts out there waiting for us to discover. We think we're getting it right—and we're probably more confident than the physicists are in their discoveries—but we acknowledge that we could be making mistakes and we might have to back up and start again from an earlier point and develop mathematics from there.

HB: It's worth emphasizing, I think, that most people have no difficulty in accepting the fact that we regularly make discoveries about the physical world. If I drop this cup and this cup moves at a certain rate, I can build a theory to explain why that cup is moving at a certain rate and what might happen if I would drop a similar cup or a different cup. And because we all believe that these cups are "out there" existing independent of us, if we're really clever we can link up how this cup is moving with, say, how the planets are moving and how other things are moving. So we can build bigger and bigger theories to give us a better framework to understand all these things that we're convinced are actually out there, that actually exist.

But when we talk about two plus three equalling five, or the notion that there are infinitely many prime numbers, we're left scratching our heads about *where*, exactly, these things are that we're talking about. They're clearly not in the physical world. So where are they?

JB: This is the embarrassing question for many of us. So, clearly they are not in the physical world, as you say. The number "2" isn't to be found anywhere in the world the way the metre stick is to be found in Paris under glass where we can go and actually examine it. If they let us, we could hold it; we could check other metre sticks to make sure they're the right length and stuff like that. Numbers aren't like that. So, the big question is, *How do we get to know anything about them? How do we grasp them? How do we see these truths?*

Well, we can't literally grasp or literally see. I can only use metaphors at this point, but there seems to be some kind of cognitive capacity that human beings actually have that they are able to understand these things and come to believe them rationally.

I don't know how it's done. It is a mystery. It's an embarrassment, frankly; and, in fact, for people who don't like Platonism, it's the number one issue to hammer a Platonist with. You just say, "*Well, how the hell do you **do** this?*"

HB: Right: How can you possibly get access to this world that's outside of space and time?

JB: Exactly. So, here is a cup on the table. And I know that the cup is on the table because photons are coming into my eye both from the cup and from the table.

Those photons interact with me, they interact with my eye in a process I call "seeing", and that has a lot to do with my knowledge. In fact, if photons weren't coming, I'd be hard-pressed to actually know anything about it.

There doesn't seem to be anything like this for mathematics. Wouldn't it be nice if there were little "Platons" coming from Plato's Heaven down into the mind's eye, as it were, that would clearly account for us seeing and grasping these mathematical truths. But, unfortunately, that seems a little preposterous. So right now, we just don't know.

HB: Let me ask you to back up a little bit for more historical context. Anyone reading this who is not a student of philosophy might say to themselves, "*Platonism—that obviously has to do with Plato—but what's that all about, exactly? How did that come to pass, historically?*"

JB: Well, Plato lived roughly 400 BCE, so let's say 2,500 years ago. For me, he is the greatest of them all. He is my hero.

Why do we call our current view "Platonism"? Well, for Plato the number one issue is this idea of abstract entities.

So, there are a lot of chairs around the room. What do they all have in common? Well, they are all examples of chairs. They have—it sounds like a silly word—they have "chair-ness" in common. And so, Plato thought that there was a kind of "form", a perfect chair, or maybe a blueprint of a chair or something like that, that has some kind of existence in its own right. In which case the actual chairs in the room are somehow "copies" or "instances" of the form. And this is the centerpiece of Platonism, this is the piece that we keep today.

There are other things that go along with Plato's actual views that are just preposterous, things that we wouldn't believe today. So, for instance, he thought that nobody learns mathematics or anything else. What they do is *remember* mathematics. For Plato, we're immortal and our souls used to exist in this thing that we call Plato's Heaven where they gazed upon the perfect circle, the perfect triangle and so on. They knew it all from direct experience there. And in the act of being born your poor brain gets jostled around and you forget everything.

And then what happens in education is we draw it out. Socratic education is the process of helping you to remember.

HB: There's this wonderful scene in the Platonic dialogue *Meno*, for example.

JB: That's right. The classic example is from the *Meno*, where the slave boy who's never been taught any mathematics at all produces a proof. And this is supposed to be evidence that he actually already knew it from his life before birth.

But no one sensible today believes in reincarnation and all of that. So we can't have that view. We have to have some other kind of epistemology—a theory about how we learn mathematics—to go along with the stuff about abstract entities. So the modern Platonist is only saying, "*The abstract entities, that's the part Plato got right.*" And that's why we call it Platonism.

HB: And as you said, for Plato, there were not only mathematical entities: there was also the idea of "chair-ness" or "cat-ness" or whatever—which might strike some people as downright silly—but there are forms that are considerably more reasonable, at least to me: things like "Beauty" or "Truth".

JB: That's right. There is a whole hierarchy of stuff up there.

HB: But in contemporary Platonism, we're only looking at the mathematical aspects of this.

JB: Yes. And there are some people in ethics who also invoke Platonism. It hasn't been popular for a while, but I think it's making a slight comeback.

HB: Oh, really?

JB: Well, they're not going whole hog on Platonism: they don't believe that you're remembering what's good, or something like that. But they do think that perhaps we have a kind of intuitive intellectual grasp of good and bad.

The wonderful thing about it, the thing that appeals to me about moral Platonism, is that it gives you moral objectivity. There's no relativity. There's a genuine objective right and wrong.

HB: There really *is* good and bad.

JB: Yes: there really is good and bad. It might be really hard to figure it out—we might not know what's good and bad any more than we know all the mathematical truths. We're just slowly discovering things. But on the other hand, there's no God involved here. God plays no role whatsoever and you have perfectly objective ethics but no divine.

HB: There are just these forms that are out there.

JB: That's right.

Questions for Discussion:

1. How might Platonistic arguments be used in the search for extraterrestrial intelligence? Readers with a particular interest in this topic are referred to the Ideas Roadshow conversation **SETI: Astronomy as a Contact Sport** *with Jill Tarter.*

2. What are some of the difficulties associated with rejecting mathematical Platonism?

II. Attacks and Defenses
Platonism under fire

HB: Let's get back to mathematics. And to preempt those who might say, *"That's just silly!"* or *"How can we seriously talk of these "forms" that we have no clear access to?"* you invoke what in your books you sometimes call "a shameless appeal to authority". You rattle off some of the greatest minds in the history of mathematics—including but by no means limited to Plato—who actually were avowed Platonists. Maybe now would be a good time to highlight some of those famous Platonists.

JB: Well, mathematicians and philosophers will recognize some of the names. We could start, for example, with Gottlob Frege, a German logician and philosopher in the late 19th, early 20th century. He was a fabulously brilliant fellow and a thoroughgoing Platonist. A great British mathematician by the name of Hardy, who was active early in the 20th century, was also a resolute Platonist, and he had nice imagery when he talked about how he did mathematics in his book, *A Mathematician's Apology*.

"*Proofs don't mean anything,*" he said, "*Proofs are just—*" I think he used the word "*gas*". They're just rhetorical flourishes, just showing off. The *real* facts, he said, are like this: "*It's as if I can see a distant mountain range and I see a peak and then a couple more peaks. And then I pull you over and say, 'I want you to just look over here. You see this peak that you already know of. Now, look a little bit to the right and just behind it. You see that thing there?' I can point out something new to you that you've never seen before. And then you'll say, 'Oh, yeah, now I get it.' And this is mathematics.*"

So, you have a kind of perception—an almost literal perception—of these mathematical truths, which exists out there independently from you.

Now, to help you see them, I might actually give you a proof. In fact, journals tend to demand them. They don't like this, "*Look at the second peak on the right*" business. They don't go for that.

HB: But at some fundamental level, according to Hardy, that's really superfluous, it's just dressing up what you've intuited in some deep way.

JB: That's right. Intuition—a kind of perception of these abstract entities—is what's really going on. And those mountain peaks, speaking metaphorically, they're *there*. They're just waiting there for you to discover them. It's a wonderful picture.

Of course, the name most people will recognize is Kurt Gödel, the famous Austrian logician. Gödel was a flat-out, unabashed Platonist. He said the only way he could make sense of mathematics was to imagine that there's a kind of intuition, a kind of perception, of mathematical objects. And he said, "*You can't make sense of mathematics without this form of perception any more than you can make sense of our physical knowledge without the fact that we've got eyesight and we can perform experiments and observe things.*" A perfect analogy, he thought.

HB: And a great living mathematical physicist who is also an unabashed Platonist is Roger Penrose.

JB: Right. And he takes very much the same view as Gödel on this question. I think he cites Gödel at length in an approving way. We're all on the same side, doing battle against the Philistines!

HB: Okay, so you've established the authoritative team that you're a member of.

JB: Absolutely.

HB: I want to move to some of your particular arguments and perspectives on Platonism because you have some unique insights that I think are very worthy of discussion.

But before I do, I'd like you to play devil's advocate a little bit. We've established that if I'm somebody who discovers a mathematical insight, a new mathematical truth, and then say, *"Aha, I just discovered this new mathematical truth!"* a sceptical non-Platonist would reply, *"Oh, that's just silly. You're not discovering anything. How could you? Even if this thing you say you're discovering somehow existed outside of space and time, how on earth could you possibly know about it?"*

So that's one negative reaction that would come my way. What might be some of the other things that a non-Platonist would say?

JB: Well, that's probably the big one.

Often you find certain general philosophical attitudes inside philosophy, and one that's very common today is called "naturalism". So, what a naturalist says, first and foremost, is that the natural sciences—physics, chemistry, biology—they're a success story. No question.

And then they might say something like, *"They are giving us knowledge. **And nothing else can**. There is no other avenue to learn anything about reality except through the natural sciences."*

Historically the alternatives have been things like the Bible—you learn about reality by reading what it says in Genesis, for instance.

Okay, so that's not on these days. Nor is reading tea leaves, and so on.

HB: But then mathematics wouldn't be a way either, presumably.

JB: Right. This makes mathematics a real problem. So, naturalists would then say, *"Okay, what we have to do to maintain our naturalism is to give an account for all these things where we like to claim we know something, that don't fit into the physics, chemistry, or biology ways of doing things."*

So that includes mathematics. It also includes morality and philosophical knowledge generally—a whole lot of stuff. And so they have to give some account. They will be desperate to do something to give some sort of account of how we might have mathematical knowledge that doesn't appeal to this, as they see it, "wild" Platonic stuff.

So they'll say, *"Wouldn't it be nice if we could have an account."* And they'll try to develop those—almost none of them are successful. John Stuart Mill in the 19th century, though he wouldn't have called himself a naturalist but maybe an updated version would, might say something like, *"It's just empiricism. You just look and count what you see. You've got two apples here. You've got three apples there. Push them together and you've got five apples."*

And according to Mill, all of our mathematical knowledge is built up in this kind of straightforward empiricist way, which means that mathematical facts, like two plus three equals five, are actually not abstract truths, but they are, in fact, truths about the world. It just means that combining any two objects with three objects gives you five material objects.

HB: Which in some ways means that it's at least logically possible to be in the world, or to be in some other world, or in another universe or somewhere, where combining two objects and three objects gives you six objects.

JB: That's right: even Mill would concede that, I think. That looks to me like a reductio ad absurdum of his view, but he's willing to bite the bullet, as it were.

Now the trouble is, even if you can make that work for very low-level arithmetic of small numbers, you run into serious problems as soon as you start talking about negative numbers or complex numbers or something like that.

Just consider, three apples minus five apples equals minus two apples. All right, Mill, show us the minus five apples and we'll see what we can do about operating with it: you run into these sorts of problems almost immediately.

Another view that's quite popular is to somehow turn it into the result of evolution. So, here's the claim: *"There is nothing deeply objective about arithmetic. It's just that people who think the way we think have tended to have children who survived. People who thought in a kind of different way have tended not to."*

HB: So mathematics is actually somehow attributable to **us**? So mathematics is just a representation of the way we think? This is the argument?

JB: That's right. It's just an expression of how we think and it's been adaptive. Basically, your ancestors said, "*My three friends and I can beat up those two guys because we outnumber them.*"

Meanwhile, those who said, "*Okay, now there are 17 of those guys and there are five of us. Oh, good, the odds are in our favour!*", tended not to have many children.

So therefore only people who think like us, who do arithmetic like us, they are the ones who tended to survive and have children and that's why we think the way we do today and why things like two plus two equals four feel so certain. It's just that we're hardwired that way.

HB: Well, that's—

JB: Yes. That's preposterous too.

HB: I certainly think so. So one kind of argument against this is that if we were ever to find an alien life form somewhere, then they would presumably use a completely different math. They wouldn't believe that three plus one necessarily equals four. Unless you had some super meta-environmental survival hypothesis that would presumably—

JB: If their environment was truly weird so that objects tended not to be stable in the way they are here, then a different kind of arithmetic might suit them. But we know from elementary chemistry that if I take one litre of water and one litre of something else and mix them together, I may not get two litres of liquid. I may get 1.9 litres of something. I can't remember why exactly...

HB: This is one of the reasons why I stopped doing chemistry.

JB: But if you lived in a world where mixing things like that was absolutely central to your existence, you might in fact have a kind of weirdo arithmetic.

HB: Sure. But at some level, as we both, I think, agree, that may work in terms of mixing things together and doing some operational things, but it wouldn't enable you to build any reasonable, consistent ideas in higher mathematics.

JB: That's certainly what I believe. I'm with you.

HB: Which, in turn, forms the basis of all of our understanding of physical law.

JB: That's right.

HB: And one could argue that's arbitrary or part of our genetic makeup, but I certainly wouldn't and neither would you. So anyway, there we go: I asked you to play devil's advocate a little bit and give me some examples. And you did. It's hardly your fault if the positions you cited were ludicrous.

Another point you mention in your books is related to the so-called "causal theory of knowledge". And at first glance, at least, it seems like a formidable criticism against Platonism.

JB: Yes. In a sense I alluded to it earlier, but I can make it very specific now. This was a very popular doctrine say 20 to 30 years ago. It's declining in its influence now but it's still out there. The idea is this: in order for me to know about anything, I actually have to causally interact with it.

Let's suppose that I know it's snowing in Moscow right now, right this minute. How do I know that? Well, I just looked at the weather report. There were photons coming off a printed page or maybe a computer screen into my eye. Well, how did it get on to the computer screen? Somebody, somewhere else, was typing something—an electronic signal came and made that image. And whoever typed it in got a message, perhaps from a phone call from some guy in Moscow, who looked out the window and felt snowflakes or saw them via photons hitting his eye, and so on. And hence there is this long chain from the actual snow in Moscow to me.

HB: Direct causal links.

JB: Direct causal links. They might be very complicated, but they need to be there. And if that chain had been broken, and no other chain established, I simply couldn't know that it was there.

There is a lot of natural plausibility to the causal theory of knowledge. And once you accept this, then you're in trouble, because you face the criticism of, "*Well, now, you claim to know mathematical truths that are mathematical facts about stuff in Plato's Heaven. That's outside space and time and you are inside. Tell me about the causal process that gets from there to here.*" And you immediately say, "*Oh, gosh, this is a really embarrassing question.*"

And I have no answer to it. Not directly. I have an indirect answer. Want to hear the indirect answer?

HB: I'd like to get there shortly. But before I do, I'd like to deal with one more piece of criticism.

Putting ourselves in the anti-Platonist camp for just a minute or two longer, so far the big arrow in our quiver is the whole issue of how we can possibly get access to this mysterious metaphysical realm of Plato's Heaven outside of space and time. I can say this generally, or I can say it more specifically using this causal theory of knowledge, but either way that's the core concern I have.

JB: Right.

HB: But there may be another piece of criticism that I may level at the situation, which is simply, *Well, who cares anyway? What difference does it make? Why should I even be worried about this? Maybe these forms are out there, maybe they're not. Maybe we'll never be able to* *determine whether these things actually exist in any sense, but math is still math so why should I be worried about that one way or the other?*

And in one of your books you gave a thoughtful refutation of this view that I think is most interesting.

Correct me if I'm wrong, but my sense is that you draw a parallel to the physical world when you say that the analogous approach to the physical world is to say, *Well, maybe this mug doesn't actually exist either. In fact, I can go right ahead and just assume that this mug **doesn't** actually exist.*

But then I get in trouble if I try to pour water in here—everything goes to hell in a hand-basket. I've got a mess on my hands. In short, then, I *can't* just "pretend things away"—there's a real effect that's actually going on here.

And similarly for the mathematical world, it's not just that we are retrodicting afterwards, saying, "*These forms are there*" based on consistency considerations or what have you. That's the wrong way of looking at the question.

The argument, the strict Platonist argument, is that the *reason* why we can intuit the fact that two plus two equals four, the reason why we have that in the first place, is because those forms actually *are* there.

JB: That's right.

HB: And if those forms weren't there, if there weren't these abstract mathematical entities representing all sorts of complex mathematical ideas, then we wouldn't have those ideas ourselves; we simply *wouldn't be able* to have them, just like we wouldn't be able to see this cup if it weren't there.

JB: That's right. I think that's exactly right.

HB: Well, they're your words, after all.

JB: Well said—or rather, well memorized.

There's an interesting old argument from George Berkeley that's somewhat analogous to all of this. Some people might find it worthwhile—and if you haven't heard of Berkeley, he's a very interesting fellow in his own right.

Anyway, Berkeley thought that everything was just sensations in us. You are a sensation in me, the table is a sensation in me, and so is the cup, and so forth. So what we think of as the table is really nothing but a cluster of different sensations: the sensation of hardness, the sensation of a spatial shape, the sensation of colour. If I were to lick it, it would have some taste to it and so on.

And we're with him so far. And then he says something truly dramatic, he says, "*And that's it. There's nothing else. There's no table out there that actually has these properties that you're detecting. All you've got are the cluster of sensations.*"

Berkeley believed in God, and there's a sense that God is necessary to hold it all together. So when we leave the room, the table, in a sense, stays because God is looking at it. But if God should just sort of nod off, it disappears.

So if I asked "*Does the tree falling in the forest make a sound if nobody hears it?*" Berkeley's answer would be, "*If nobody hears it, it just doesn't make a sound.*" Meanwhile the rest of us say, "*Oh, sure it does. We just don't hear it.*"

Now, the common-sense reply to Berkeley is, "*Well, you have to explain something. You have to explain why you think there is a table here, why you think there is a chair over there, why you think there is a cup here and so do I.*" So how do we get this commonality? The obvious, easy answer is there really is a table there and it's causing your sensations and mine.

HB: Sure.

JB: Now, when it comes to mathematical intuitions, think of it like a kind of perception. The best explanation for the fact that our intuitions match—I mean *really* match; it's remarkable how stable mathematical intuitions are over a long period of time—

HB: As well as over wide geographical areas, across all sorts of different people who are anthropologically very distinct.

JB: That's right. It's culturally pretty stable from culture to culture, and it's pretty stable over a long period of time from person to person. There's nothing else like it. I mean, sometimes people try to embarrass mathematical Platonists by saying, "*Well, so we're seeing God, are we? Having a religious experience?*"

But actually, religious experiences are *nowhere near* as stable and as common from person to person the way the feeling that two plus three equals five is just so obviously solid. You just can't shake it.

So how do you explain that? The best explanation seems to be that there is a common thing that's independent from us that you intuit and I intuit, just like the common cup here on this table that you see and I see.

HB: In other words, two plus three *really does* equal five.

JB: It really does.

HB: And what we mean by "really does equal five" is that somehow, just like that cup is there, it's there too.

JB: It's there. It's part of reality in this larger sense. It's not part of the physical reality, but it's part of reality.

HB: One of the things that has always impressed me about you is that you go into this very tricky thicket and you move forth in a very open and straightforward way. As you mentioned before, there are others who do or did this—Roger Penrose and Gödel and so forth—but it's still worth mentioning, I think, that you have the courage of your convictions to go boldly into sometimes dodgy metaphysical waters with full knowledge of the perils and counter-arguments which are sometimes quite significant. But you say up front, "*No, this is what I believe. This must be true. It's absurd to think anything other than this,*" and then you go off to develop arguments to support your views—and I want to get to some of those arguments very soon.

And that has long struck me as noteworthy, because in my experiences, encountering people from various different academic communities, this issue seemed particularly marked by a general sense of shameful levels of hypocrisy and doublethink. In particular, it seemed very common for most mathematicians to be what I called "Platonists by day and formalists by night"—or perhaps it was the other way around, given how many work at night—but my point is that, in their day job, working away on some paper, they believed quite strongly that they were making discoveries. And when they'd come up with something new or significant, they would consequentially be, quite understandably, very proud of the fact that they'd discovered a theorem.

JB: Yes.

HB: And they'd believe very strongly and sincerely that what they're doing when they make a discovery is not at all dissimilar to what a physicist or chemist or a biologist or anyone in the natural sciences is doing when they make a discovery.

JB: That's right.

HB: And this gut feeling, this intuition, this core belief, is widespread throughout the mathematical community, independent of culture, gender, geography and what have you.

And yet, if you'd go to a cocktail party, meet a mathematician and ask her, "*Well, are there really these mathematical objects that exist out there? Is it really true that that's what you're doing?*", she'll invariably hum and haw and say something like, "*That's metaphysics. Leave that to the philosophers. I don't know.*"

They'll scale things down because, of course, they recognize the conceptual difficulties, the metaphysical difficulties. They would have to then say, as a logical consequence of this, "*There's this separate realm of reality that I can't explain how we get access to,*" and all the rest. They'll naturally shy away from that. And that's always struck me as pretty craven, quite frankly.

I mean, they'll use these weasel words and equivocate, but at the end of the day if you're a mathematician, your job, your career, your life, is all about doing mathematics.

So perhaps I'm being heavy-handed here, but I think that there's a certain ethical issue at play: if you're a mathematician and you really are a Platonist—I mean, if you don't believe that, if you really believe you're manipulating symbols all day long, fair enough—but if you really are, indeed, a Platonist, then I think you should come out of the closet and be prepared to announce to all and sundry, "*I'm a Platonist. Maybe there are lots of things that I don't understand about this philosophy, but I really believe that this must be true.*"

Anyway, you do this, at least. So good for you.

JB: Well, thank you. But now I'm going to be devil's advocate.

HB: Again?

JB: Again.

HB: Okay.

JB: I could imagine somebody taking the following view: "*I find it extremely productive in my work to act like a Platonist, as if these things are there and I'm discovering them. Now, the real truth? I'm not sure. But it's a really good way to work. But when I stand back and look at it, then I have to express a bit of scepticism.*"

Here's an analogy. Suppose you're learning navigation in the days prior to GPS. You want to sail your boat around the world or something. Do you know what people were taught in order to navigate? Ptolemaic astronomy. It was known to be false, but very useful nonetheless.

So they'd say, "*Okay, I know this isn't the way things really are, but it's incredibly good and it gets me from point A to point B and with the minimum of mistakes and minimal calculation, and so on.*"

You could imagine something just like that in circumstances where we didn't know the truth about astronomy, with somebody saying, *"Well, I do it in this Ptolemaic way and I'm not confident that it's really true, but I find it very useful to act as if it were true when I'm navigating because what I really care about is the navigation."*

HB: Okay, Mr Devil's Advocate.

JB: Yes?

HB: I have a problem with this.

JB: Wasn't I generous to my enemies?

HB: You were very generous. But let me take your straw devil's advocate man and try to blow him down.

JB: Okay.

HB: Here's my problem with the analogy. The problem is that there really *is* something worthwhile and meaningful to the idea of navigating from point A to point B. So the question of how precisely to do it is clearly a means to an end. We all agree that the real, fundamental issue—the only thing that really matters—is to figure out how to get from point A to point B. How exactly we get there, we don't really care about.

So this analogy would similarly imply that there really is something real and fundamental in obtaining—we would naturally say discovering—a new theorem. But if you don't believe in Platonism, then that doesn't work. If you don't believe in Platonism, there's not really anything real or fundamental going on, because you're not, in fact, "discovering" anything at all—you're just manipulating symbols around.

JB: Yes. Enlarging the fictions.

HB: Right. Now suppose you were to approach a mathematician who was a Platonist by day and a cocktail party sceptic by night and ask, *"Is it a reasonable thing to just be manipulating symbols all day according to one game of chess, and somebody else could do it according to chess prime, or chess double prime, a different sort of game with correspondingly different rules?"*

Because it seems to me that if they really started believing that that's, in fact, all they're doing—just manipulating symbols around—then they would quickly lose their motivation for doing it.

JB: Yes. I certainly would. But I suspect that you and I see the world the same way, that we're interested in how things really are. And if it turns out that there isn't a way things really are, that it's nothing but a body of fictions, then rather than trying to contribute to the body of fictions—which some people are very happy to do—we would simply say, *"No, I'm not interested in playing."* I would probably say, *"I'll go do something else. I'll just leave mathematics aside. I'll go and do physics where I'm actually figuring out how the world works."*

Now, this is something that you can't really argue about. It's more like a matter of taste. I mean, there are a lot of fictions that I love, like literature.

HB: Sure.

JB: I don't expect my novels to be true.

HB: Yes, but the author isn't pretending that they're true either.

JB: That's right. He isn't even trying.

Questions for Discussion:

1. Do you agree with Howard that it is "unethical" for a mathematician to not admit to his "working Platonist assumptions"?

2. Which of this chapter's arguments against Platonism did you find most persuasive? Which one did you find least persuasive?

III. Seeing With the Mind's Eye
Two revealing examples

HB: Anyway, I've taken you too far afield, because the real point that I was trying to make was simply that I had great respect for the fact that you strongly adhere to your deep convictions, fully aware of the fact that there are serious metaphysical difficulties associated with them.

And then, on top of that, you actually try to address them. You think about concrete ways of dealing with them rather than just avoiding them or saying, "*That's extremely difficult.*"

We were speaking about how the principal problem with Platonism is this notion of how we get access to knowledge in this strange metaphysical world that is out of space and time, how we intuit these mathematical truths which are out there.

You've spent a great deal of time looking closely at the notion of thought experiments. Presumably one of your motivations in doing that was to get a firmer handle on just what this Platonic intuition might be and how it might work.

JB: Right. Well, it's clear that, in the history of physics, thought experiments have played a huge role, from ancient times up to the present day.

Some of the most famous are from the time of the scientific revolution when Galileo and Newton performed thought experiments that were really central and revolutionary in many ways. And then, of course, in relativity you've got Einstein's thought experiments involving the elevator and running after a beam of light. There is Heisenberg's gamma ray thought experiment, which gives you the famous uncertainty principle. There's Schrödinger's Cat. They're just endless.

It's really an interesting question how they work. I mean, the fundamental problem of thought experiments is, *How is it possible, just by thinking, that we can learn something new about the world?*

Now, the ordinary view about how humans acquire knowledge is through the senses. We have to go out and look if we're going to acquire something new.

And yet it seems that with thought experiments we can actually, somehow or other, get a handle on something brand new that we didn't know before, and we seem to have done it almost through magic.

So here's a simple example. Imagine Galileo at the top of the Leaning Tower of Pisa—it's unclear whether or not he actually performed this, by the way. Some historians say yes and others say no.

HB: What's your view?

JB: Well, my view would be amateurish. But I hope he didn't, because then the thought experiment did it all. There are places in the text where he says, "*I don't need to do it because I know what's going to happen,*" which makes him sound like he doesn't want to perform actual experiments.

So anyway, here's the background. According to Aristotle, as well as common sense, there's a notion that heavy things fall faster than light things. This conforms to our experience, right?

HB: More or less.

JB: Okay, so you imagine yourself—and I do mean *imagine*—on top of the Leaning Tower of Pisa and you're dropping little musket balls and big cannon balls.

Aristotle says heavy things are going to fall faster than light things, so if you drop them together the cannon ball will hit earlier. So let's accept that, as a principle, heavy things fall faster than light things.

Now, let's stick the two things together: you've got a light musket ball and a heavy cannon ball stuck together somehow, maybe with a small piece of chewing gum or glue or something.

When we drop this combination of the two balls stuck together, the two of them are heavier than the heavy cannonball by itself. So that means that, by Aristotle's rule, it ought to fall *faster* than the cannonball by itself.

But the trouble is, you can also look at it the other way: the heavy cannonball wants to go really fast, but the light musket ball wants to go slower, so it's acting like a little drag. It's like a little mini parachute on the cannon ball. It's going to slow it down. So that means that the combined object is going to fall *slower* than the heavy cannon ball all by itself.

Now you've got an absurdity.

HB: A contradiction.

JB: That's right. It's both faster and slower, which is absurd. So that's the end of Aristotle's position on this issue. It simply can't be right.

But now the obvious solution to the problem just wants to reach out and grab you by the throat: *Everything has to fall at exactly the same rate*—heavy, light, composite, uniform objects, it makes no difference. They all must fall at exactly the same rate.

That's a *stupendous* discovery by Galileo and it's all done in his head.

HB: So, as you pointed out, there are two remarkably things that are going on. The first is that you've reached a contradiction. You found that your old premises and your old way of thinking must be wrong.

JB: That's right.

HB: But there is something else. You've got a very clearly suggested path to what the true answer must be.

JB: Exactly.

HB: Without doing one experiment.

JB: Not a single one. At least nothing new. Of course, you have to bring background experience from the past. But you haven't done anything new.

And, in fact, if you'd actually *perform* an experiment, it would get in the way, because the unfortunate fact is that heavy things often *do* fall faster than light things, because of air resistance or what have you.

HB: So there's an argument for not performing any experiments right there.

JB: That's right. One of my favourite historians of science is the French thinker Alexandre Koyré. The usual view of the scientific revolution in the 16th and 17th centuries is that people started to actually go out and perform experiments, whereas prior to that they were just armchair philosophers, trying to think about how the world worked.

But Koyré says, "*No. That's exactly backward. The medievals were out there performing experiments all over the damned place, and what happened with Galileo is that people stopped **looking** and started **thinking**.*" He loved Galileo, and he thought Galileo was a hero because of thought experiments. Galileo was doing a priori physics.

HB: And that's the opposite view from what's being taught and being passed down in our schools.

JB: That's right.

HB: I know this is your favourite thought experiment. And, in fact, you like it so much that you gave it the name "Platonic", or at least put it squarely in the category of a number of what you call "Platonic thought experiments".

JB: Yes.

HB: But there are also some pure mathematical thought experiments. This one about Galileo and the balls is particularly interesting because it gives us an a priori way of intuiting the way the physical world works, as you've stressed, but from a metaphysical point of view, we already know the physical world is actually out there—well, most of us do, anyway.

So there are very important questions, as you say, about how we go about gaining knowledge of this external world, but the question we're trying to address here is: How might we better understand or explain this notion of grasping *mathematical* truths in the mind's eye—this notion of intuition?

JB: Yes.

HB: And you have some examples that can shed valuable light on this as well.

JB: Examples of visual reasoning in mathematics, yes. One which I've always found extremely impressive is a picture proof of a very simple theorem in number theory.

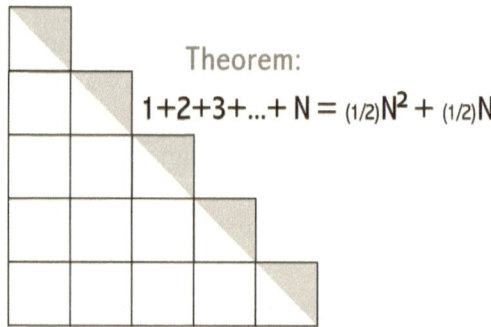

The theorem says that the expression: $1 + 2 + 3 + \ldots + N$, where the number 'N' can be any number you like, is equal to $N^2/2 + N/2$.

In other words: $1 + 2 + 3 + \ldots + N = N^2/2 + N/2$.

Now if we look at the top left part of the picture—forget about the shading for a moment—and start counting the rows, you will count off one square, then two squares, then three squares, four squares, five squares, and so forth.

So that's clearly the left side of the equation: $1 + 2 + 3 + \ldots + N$ for N=5.

Now, study that picture for just a moment and look at the form on the right-hand side of the theorem: $N^2/2 + N/2$.

Take a look at the first term, $N^2/2$. That would be a square with all sides of length N cut in half with a diagonal. Again, in our case N=5, so it's half of the 25 squares marked out by the diagonal, or rather, all the squares and bits of squares you see in the picture in white.

Meanwhile, the second term on the right hand side, $N/2$, is represented by the dark bits added in, which for N=5 total up to 2½ squares.

So it's clear, visually, that the theorem is true, that the total number of squares, independent of the colour—the left-hand side of the equation, $1 + 2 + 3 + \ldots + N$, equals the white bits, $N^2/2$, plus the black bits, $N/2$.

But if you look at that diagram, you see how powerful it is because when you see how the diagram works, you understand how the equation works generally. You see that it works not just for N=5, but N=6 as well. It works for N=20. It works for every single number N, all infinitely many of them.

And that's truly remarkable. I don't know exactly what's going on that allows us to see the truth of that theorem just by looking at that diagram, but when you've studied it long enough you become convinced of two things: first, that it actually *is* a proof. I mean, a *real* proof. The normal proof of this is by a process called mathematical induction, which everyone is happy to accept. The normal ideology of mathematics is that you should stay away from pictures. They can be psychologically helpful, but they're not actual evidence.

HB: You need a "real proof".

JB: That's right. The thinking is, *You need a real proof and the picture isn't a real proof*. But when you've studied something like that, when you look at that example, you begin to think, *No, that's a real proof.*

That does it. That's just as convincing. The evidence is every bit as strong in favour of that theorem from that picture as a "normal" proof.

HB: It makes me think of what you said earlier about Hardy pointing to the mountain peaks.

JB: Yes, certainly.

HB: "*I can do it with induction. I could do it with pictures. I could do it this way. I could do it that way. But I've glimpsed it.*"

JB: Yes. You've got some kind of real grasp of the independent mathematical reality.

HB: Exactly. All this other stuff is just words or things that I can dress it up with to try to convince you if you can't someone see it, but looking at that picture, I've got it.

JB: You can see it. And if you said, "*Oh, I see that it works for 5, but I'm not sure about 13. Show me 13,*" then we'd say, "*No, no, you haven't got it yet. Let's study the N=5 case a bit longer and then the light will go on. At some point the light will go on and then you'll see that it works for every single number N.*"

HB: Right. So this isn't a "proof" of Platonism, in the sense that it doesn't enable me to say, "*Ah! Now I've explicitly solved the problem of how I can get access to this world outside of space and time.*" But it is nonetheless very suggestive in that it gives some insight into at least some of the ways that we do get this access.

You've been able to isolate, it seems to me, the sense of this "glimpsing", develop a freeze frame of our moment of access to mathematical truths, without necessarily understanding precisely how it all works.

JB: "Glimpse" is a nice term here. Somehow or other you have that little bit of perception, that little grasp, that little seeing with the mind's eye.

Questions for Discussion:

1. Why do you think the standard view of Galileo's role in the scientific revolution is so misguided?

2. Do you agree that the picture provided in this chapter is "just as convincing" as a more formal mathematical proof of the theorem?

3. Why do you think Jim brought up the example of Galileo and the falling balls? What, if any, are the implications of this for how we should develop our theories of physics?

IV. Platonism Bounces Back
From quantum physics to the mind-body problem

HB: Earlier I stopped you when you wanted to talk about your particular—well, refutation may be too strong—let's say your particular solution to the problem presented to Platonism by the causal theory of knowledge.

And I'd like to return to that now. Just to briefly recap, the argument put forward by those who subscribe to the causal theory of knowledge is that, according to Platonism, there's this land outside of space and time, which clearly can't be causally connected to us in the normal sense. And since those who subscribe to the causal theory of knowledge say that all knowledge we have must be causally connected to us, in their view Platonism simply can't work.

JB: That's right. The general claim is that you can't know anything unless you're causally connected to it.

HB: But now you combat this view using physics.

JB: Yes. I mean, quantum mechanics is so interesting and bizarre that you can almost always find an example in quantum mechanics that will solve any problem for you.

HB: It won't help you with understanding the foundations of quantum mechanics, though.

JB: No, that's right. But anyway, the argument goes like this: if we could show that we actually *have* knowledge in the ordinary physical world without a causal connection, that would undermine the causal theory of knowledge.

There are various quite strange situations that have been studied for quite a while now in the foundations of physics, and they stem from the thought experiment first put forward by Einstein, Podolsky and Rosen in the 1930s, which is now naturally referred to as the "EPR experiment" after its three authors.

They imagine—well it's not exactly their example but a later version of their example, but anyway it's the same basic idea—that you've got a source in the middle of your laboratory that will send out a pair of photons over to detectors at each wing of the experimental apparatus that are typically at least several metres apart.

And each detector has something like a Polaroid filter on it, and we'll orient the filters the same way so that if a photon makes it through the one on one end it will not be able to make it through the one on the other end. They're perfectly correlated. Now, we can set up an experiment like this.

And Einstein and his colleagues said, "*Well, obviously, this correlation is set right at the beginning: that photon is coming out oriented this way and the other photon is coming out oriented that way and that's why you get this perfect correlation.*"

Now it may be chancy. This one could come out down and the other one up, or the other way around, but you'll always get this correlation, because it's fixed right at the origin.

HB: And the thinking is that these correlations are set initially, they exist even before you make a measurement, even before you look at them.

JB: Even before you look, right. The measurements don't in any way "create" them. Einstein, Podolsky and Rosen gave a really brilliant argument for that; and in their day I would have found that completely persuasive.

Now, in the '60s, another physicist, John Bell, came along. He loved this argument, but he thought there may be a flaw in it. Anyway, what he did was generalize from the straight up case of the Polaroid filter being oriented in the same way, saying, "*Let's start randomizing them here, put them in different ways and see what the correlations come out as. If Einstein & Co. are right, then there should be a certain statistical distribution."*

So measurements, experiments have been performed—some of them very subtle—and it turns out that Einstein and his colleagues were wrong: it can't be right. Bell suspected it was wrong and in that sense his suspicion was confirmed.

So there are two things at issue.

One is this idea that the settings of what we measure are fixed from the start, right at the origin, if we hold onto the other thing, which is that nothing can travel faster than the speed of light. That's the other assumption in the argument.

If I'm over here at one wing of the apparatus and I'm rotating my detector at random when the photon is half-way along towards me, which means that the detector here doesn't have enough time to tell the detector on the other side what its setting is in such a way to save the correlation statistics by somehow hooking up with the other side of the experimental apparatus.

So there are two assumptions: There is a way the world is right from the start—the settings, the properties these particles had before they went on their way in opposite directions—and nothing travels faster than the speed of light.

And these two assumptions together lead to this thing called Bell's inequality, which is experimentally refuted. That means that at least one of the two assumptions, one of the two initial premises has to go. And the one that goes for many people is that these eventually measurable properties of the photons were fixed, they were determined, at the origin.

And the upshot to all that is that if you're on one side of the EPR apparatus and you detect the spin is up, it makes it through the filter, then you will be able to *immediately* predict what the outcome is on the other side, far away from you.

HB: You know.

JB: That's right, you know. You know what the outcome on the other side of the apparatus is. But there cannot be any causal connection from one wing of the apparatus to the other unless something can go faster than the speed of light.

And if we insist that that can't happen, then you know something about something that's going on in the world that you are not causally connected to it.

HB: So, this is a counterexample.

JB: That's right. It's a counterexample to the causal theory of knowledge.

HB: So just to recap: the causal theory of knowledge says, "*The only way you can ever know anything is if you are in causal contact with it*", and the physicist would say, "*Well, the only way you could be in causal contact with it is if it's in your light cone, if it's within a distance that you don't need to go faster than the speed of light to reach, or to have been reached by it.*" That's what it means to be causally connected to it according to our understanding of physics.

JB: That's right.

HB: And so, while the proponents of the causal theory of knowledge would say, "*Platonism must be false because you've got this Platonic world outside of space and time and you can't be causally connected to it,*" you'd simply reply, "*Well, I can demonstrate that your causal theory of knowledge must be false because there are things happening in the real world that I can know while not actually being causally connected to them.*"

JB: That's right. That's the idea. Now, of course, as you can imagine, lots of people will not take arguments like this at face value. They'll challenge them. A lot of people worry that special relativity is false, that there are actually superluminal connections from one side to the other. That's actually increasingly common.

HB: I've always been confused by the people that have said, "*Well, maybe we've got superluminal connections,*" because even if you somehow *have* superluminal connections (which is, of course, a positively enormous "if"), even if it's somehow logically possible to have these connections, it doesn't really help in lots of ways.

Because then you open up this whole bizarre line of questioning: *How*, exactly, are they communicating? *What* are they communicating? How are these photons signalling to one and another? I mean, it almost doesn't even need superluminal impediments to be completely absurd.

JB: In fact, that's a really good point because I think we could respond to someone who says, *"Look, there might be a superluminal connection so you're causally connected after all,"* by saying, *"Strictly speaking, the causal theory of knowledge says more than that you have to be causally connected. It also says 'and it has to be the right kind of causal connection,' not just 'anything'."*

Photons will work because you know that's related to your sense perceptions and so on. But in the case of these supposed superluminal connections, if they exist in quantum non-local situations, they're completely uncontrollable: there is no way we can control the data. You can't send signals with it.

HB: Right.

JB: That would suggest that, even if there *is* a causal connection from one side to the other, it wouldn't be the right sort of causal connection to save the causal theory of knowledge. But that makes the argument more complicated.

And so, I think the safe thing to say is that everyone should be sceptical of the causal theory of knowledge. But whether or not it can be saved from arguments like this is sort of an open question.

HB: There is another thing that you say as well, which I think is worth highlighting at this point. Naively there is a sense that, for example, we know about this cup because we have photons coming into our eye, and we do understand those processes pretty well. We have an electronic signal that comes through our optic nerve to some parts of our brain and so on. And these processes are all physiological. They're physical. They may be very complicated, they may be very difficult to isolate, but we understand them more or less in principle as opposed to this weird business of getting access to Plato's Heaven and these forms and how we know that two plus three is five and all that.

But you make an interesting point when you point out, *"Yeah, **that** part we get, but we still don't understand how all this physiological, physical stuff—signals going from here to there through this nerve or that passageway—somehow leads to our mental image of the cup, our psychological belief and conscious awareness of the fact that there is a cup on the table right now—**that** we actually don't understand at all."*

JB: We have a name for it, in fact: "the mind-body problem". You put your finger on it exactly. The problem is I don't know how many hundreds of thousands of years old. *How do the mind and the body interact with one another?* That's the problem.

In fact, what we know about the case of perception is, in fact, exactly what you said: we know about the photons entering the eyeball, interacting with the rods and cones, the signal down the optic nerve into the visual cortex and so on, but then how belief is formed is a complete and utter mystery.

I have lots of friends in cognitive science, and they would bristle at me saying that, *"It's a complete and utter mystery."* They'd say, *"No it's not! We sort of know quite a few things, actually."* But I claim they don't; they don't know a damn thing.

And so that means we're actually on a par. Of course, that's why I made the joke about "Platons" earlier. There was never a question about actual Platons entering the mind's eye. But that's not even so much the core issue.

The real mystery, in the case of math, is how we get into a psychological state of having beliefs about numbers. And I think that's no more mysterious than in the ordinary physical case, where we don't have any idea of how we have beliefs about that coffee cup. We're both in bad shape. They need to do stuff to figure out what's going on. I need to do stuff to figure out what's going on. But I'm no worse off than they are.

HB: Which is an important point to emphasize. I mean, clearly, it's not what you wanted. What you wanted was to show a concrete proof, or demonstration, or whatever, of some of the problems that are bothering you in Platonism, not to illustrate how your failings are not much worse than other people.

But it is somewhat comforting psychologically to realize that what we think we have a complete understanding of, or what we take on faith, we actually *don't* understand nearly as well even in the cases that we're making direct comparisons with.

JB: No, we don't.

Questions for Discussion:

1. Do you agree that Jim's invocation of the EPR experiment refutes the causal theory of knowledge?

2. Will the "mind-body problem" ever be solved? How might it be possible to solve it even in principle?

V. The Philosophical Life
On sociological divides and being a team player

HB: In your book, *Laboratory of the Mind*, you give a Platonic interpretation of quantum theory, which is fascinating and I would very much urge other people to look at it, but we don't have time to delve into it here. But it does bring up a more general issue for me, which is that you have a natural predilection to look at contemporary, or near contemporary, issues in theoretical physics to try to somehow harness their power and use them to address some of these arguments, ideas and concepts in philosophy.

I've often wondered how that sits with other members of the philosophical community. Do they think, *There goes Jim again, rattling on about the EPR experiment and foundational physics, trying to prove everything in the world through his own particular quantum hobbyhorse.*

Is that the sort of reaction you typically get? Or is there more appreciation for the merits of your approach? Is there a sense among fellow philosophers that, say, you've really thrown a spike deep into the heart of the causal theory of knowledge with your invocation of Einstein-Podolsky-Rosen? Or is it brushed aside as simply *"Jim doing his thing"*?

JB: Let me make a more general comment in answer to the question. There's a kind of not-entirely-happy state of affairs in contemporary philosophy. The philosophers of science are often quite close to particular sciences and the mainstream philosophers who do metaphysics and epistemology are often quite divorced from those sciences. So we tend to talk past one another. We tend to have different problems.

People in mainstream metaphysics and epistemology will talk about the nature of time or the nature of causation, but they talk about it in highly abstract terms that usually make little or no connection with contemporary science. For me, that's a real tragedy.

Often the work that these people do is unquestionably brilliant—some of the most brilliant people alive today work in mainstream metaphysics and epistemology. And the people in the philosophy of science are often nowhere near as sophisticated when they're talking about certain kinds of concepts of knowledge or causation and so on. But the thing is, they're usually grounded with real examples of what, in an ordinary sense, I would call knowledge.

I mean, if there is anything we're sure about it's that the sciences have given us knowledge—I don't want to say that I'm sure it's knowledge in the sense that we might not overthrow it tomorrow, so let me simply call it "justified belief".

We have wonderful justified beliefs given to us by physics and biology and other fields, but mainstream metaphysics and epistemology tend to talk about highly artificial examples, which just don't connect. So we pass by one another. It's a pity. We have different languages, different concerns.

I mean, I'll say, *"Well, what about this?"*, and they'll reply with something like, *"Yes, that's very interesting, but I don't have to worry about that because I'm working at a different level,"* or whatever.

It can be frustrating. Both sides are a bit frustrated. Like many pure mathematicians and many physicists, they just tend to talk past one another.

Now, there's some really good stuff where they do overlap. That's really highly fruitful, and I really like that sort of thing. By analogy, if we can get more people in philosophy of science to interact with people in mainstream philosophy and use some of their highly sophisticated, but so far not applicable notions, and somehow or other make them work in philosophy of science, I think we'd be much better off. And I'm convinced that they would be a hell of a lot better off if they paid more attention to real-world examples.

HB: Is it moving in that direction?

JB: No.

HB: Is it moving in the other direction? Is the gulf widening?

JB: I don't know if it's widening, but it's certainly not narrowing. How wide the gulf is I don't know, but it's too wide as it is, whatever it is.

HB: In terms of the people who *do* speak your language, in terms of the people who are at least prone to be influenced to some extent by your writings and your thoughts, do you think that you've had much in the way of impact? After all, you've been talking about these concepts and developing these ideas, combining thought experiments, Platonism and related issues in the philosophy of mathematics and philosophy of science, for quite some time now. Have you found that you're gaining ground or gaining converts?

JB: Winning converts? No, I wouldn't say that.

I have a very good friend, a colleague who works on thought experiments too. His name is John Norton, and he holds a completely different view than I do. He is sort of an extreme empiricist while I'm an extreme Platonist rationalist.

Nobody believes him and nobody believes me, but we're both incredibly useful to the community because many articles on thought experiments will start out and say, *There are these fruitcake views—they're wrong, of course—and I'm going to do something sensible in-between.* So we're useful foils

HB: You're establishing the intellectual terrain.

JB: That's right.

HB: Have you always found yourself on that "lunatic fringe", as it were, that Platonist rationalist boundary? Were you a Platonist as long as you can remember?

JB: Well, to be a Platonist in physics is to be considered close to the lunatic fringe, yes. In mathematics, not so. In mathematics, Platonism is—well, as you know, working mathematicians are Platonists and they have a lot of sympathy for it. And a big chunk of philosophers of mathematics are Platonists. Maybe they'll try to qualify it a little, but it's considered a perfectly respectable view.

My views are slightly unusual inside the philosophy of mathematics community, not so much for being a Platonist, but for taking pictures so seriously and emphasizing visual reasoning. But I noticed that there are a lot more people working on visual reasoning now. It's coming into a kind of fashion.

HB: So maybe you have had some influence there.

JB: I don't know. Perhaps. It may be just a coincidence.

HB: In terms of your own particular Platonic evolution, have you evolved at all? We've known each other some time and my sense is that you've been remarkably consistent in your views.

JB: Yes, I think that's true.

HB: Did you have a Platonic epiphany when you were three years old playing with pebbles on a beach or something? Did you say to yourself something like, "*This whole abstraction thing people talk about must be garbage: pebble one, pebble two. It must be up there somewhere.*"? Do you remember the first time you became aware of your Platonic resolve, as it were?

JB: Not really. I do still remember the first time I fell in love with thought experiments. I can pinpoint that. I think I got interested in math, seriously interested in math, as an undergraduate. And then, in thinking about these issues, Platonism just seemed like—

HB: The natural next step.

JB: Yes, the natural thing. And I just sort of fell into it.

In the case of thought experiments, I was just a beginning philosophy student, probably in my first or second year. And like every philosophy student, I took the standard sort of introduction to the field, where you read some rationalist philosophers: a bit of Plato, maybe a bit of Descartes. They think that you can have a priori knowledge of the world. And that's usually taught in a philosophy course only to knock it down.

Then you read the empiricists. You read Hume. Hume's wonderful, of course. So I'm reading this and thinking, *Well, Hume is very interesting—sort of—but he can't hold a candle to Descartes and Plato. But, of course, sadly, I'm sure empiricism is the truth. What a pity.*

And then somebody, one of my teachers in fact, just in an off-handed way—he wasn't trying to get us interested in thought experiments, he was talking about something else—said, *"Oh, and then Galileo did this..."* and he gave me that example.

HB: The falling balls from the Leaning Tower of Pisa.

JB: Right: the falling balls. And I was just *stupefied*. I'd never seen anything so dazzling and beautiful in all my life.

It was the most—you know, every now and then you have an intellectual experience where the light goes on? This was like a thousand light bulbs going on at the same time—it was like **the sun**! Just face to face with the sun. I'd never seen anything so spectacular in my life. And it just knocked the tar out of Hume right there.

HB: I've got one more question for you. I'm pretty sure I've asked you this before, but I can't remember what you told me, so I'm going to ask it again. And if you change your response, I won't know.

So, without going into Popper and all of that in any detail, there's a general understanding that if we're going to be genuinely scientific and make progress, we should structure things in such a way as to be able to recognize, at least in principle, that our theories might be incorrect—this notion of falsifiability.

JB: Sure.

HB: So with that in mind, my question is this: What could conceivably come along tomorrow that would make you say, "*Platonism seemed completely reasonable to me for a very long time, but I no longer believe it; it's just not true.*"?

In other words, is there anything you could even imagine occurring or experiencing that would lead to you changing your view on Platonism?

JB: Well, this will have to be pretty vague, I'm afraid.

HB: That's fine. Under the circumstances, it hardly seems reasonable to demand precision.

JB: If you could show me that Platonism as a philosophical doctrine was actually getting in the way of further mathematical developments, if it was sort of constraining mathematicians from doing certain kinds of things, then I'd have serious worries about it.

I hope I'm not dogmatic about it, but I may well be. There are lots of things that count as certain in life—including most of mathematics—that I'm not prepared to claim, in fact, are certain at all.

So, for instance, I think mathematics is highly fallible. And while it's been pretty stable, there *are* actually changes in the history of mathematics that have been rather revolutionary. A couple of hundred years ago, there was a theorem that said that every function is continuous. And certainly nobody would believe that today.

It's not because somebody made a mistake in the proof. It's rather that we have re-conceptualized the idea of a function, what counts as a function. And it was fruitful for mathematics to change that definition and allow things to develop in a different way. The prior definition was too constraining, it really amounted to something like: *A function is either a polynomial or one of the trigonometric functions*—and they are all continuous, of course.

But we now want something much more general than that. So in that sense, a piece of mathematics, a theorem like, *All functions are continuous*, is now garbage; it's wrong.

It's part of the history of mathematics, but we don't believe it. And if I thought that Platonism were somehow or other like that, or forcing people to think along lines like that—as convinced as I am of it today—I would probably abandon it.

But you know, it just occurred to me; I actually have a second ideology.

HB: Oh, you do?

JB: Yes. And that is, the way I think of science is not as a bunch of individuals trying to figure things out; I think of it as very much a *community* trying to figure things out.

It is therefore very useful to have a variety of views. So even if I thought, *Oh, Platonism is probably pretty stupid*, if there was nobody else working on it—

HB: Oh, come on! Now I've lost all respect for you, after all this time.

JB: *I remember now!* You *did* ask me this question before. I gave you the same answer and you hated it!

HB: So you're saying that you would wilfully be a hypocrite?

JB: No, no. Not a hypocrite. I couldn't work on it if I thought it was flat-out false.

HB: OK.

JB: But I *could* work on it if I thought, *It's a contender, and these other views are contenders, maybe even slightly more plausible than mine, but I want to be a good team player.*

HB: And would you come clean with this? Would you say exactly what you're saying now, in public?

JB: Oh, sure.

HB: Or would you pretend to somehow believe that yours was still the leading contender even if you thought that others were better contenders? Because, of course, if you say, "*Well, I'm going to defend this view, but I think that others are maybe even stronger contenders,*" then you're naturally minimizing your opportunity to "contribute to the greater welfare of the team", aren't you?

JB: Well, no. It can be very useful to have, as I say—

HB: Look, ***I'm*** not going to take you seriously if you stand up and say, "*I believe in this view. Well, it's probably not the strongest view. Actually…*"

JB: "*… Actually it's known to be false. But I'm on the program in this nice city in Europe thanks to my ludicrous views!*"

HB: Exactly. And, "*I'm going to represent it **because no one else will**.*"

JB: Okay. Fair enough. It may be a problem for the individuals who take that view. But you probably support that way of funding science.

You know, even the Pentagon—they don't do it anymore—but I understand that they used to fund ESP research, not because they believed it was true, but because the Russians were doing it. And they thought that there was an infinitesimally small chance that it could be right, and that people with the appropriate thought processes might change the trajectories of intercontinental ballistic missiles and turn our rockets back on us. And the thinking was, *If that's the case, we want to be there first to figure it out.*

HB: So this is some kind of portfolio-theory argument you're making.

JB: Yeah, I suppose it is.

HB: Well, I'm disappointed.

JB: But the happy news is that I am rock-solid on this one. I'm right and the rest of them are all wrong.

HB: Well, that's perfect. I'm much happier when you say that. And before I let you go, you said a few moments ago that you hoped that you weren't dogmatic.

I'm not sure what you meant by that, but for me, at least, being dogmatic means that you are unwilling to listen to reason, that you are unwilling to countenance the possibility that you might be wrong and that you're unwilling to engage in an analytical discussion of your views that could potentially lead to their downfall. That hardly strikes me as your attitude.

JB: I'm happy to say I'm not dogmatic in that sense. Maybe there's another sense: in spite of apparent goodwill, nevertheless being blind to seeing things that others, in fact, could see.

I just mean, I'm sort of set in my ways in such a way that you could give me a terrific argument against my views, but somehow or other, I'm just—try as I might—I'm psychologically incapable of seeing it.

HB: But you can't be held responsible if you're psychologically incapable, can you?

JB: Probably not. I don't know. But on the other hand, maybe we're all responsible for making sure that, when we think there might be some impediment to how we're listening to other people, we make some effort to try to see things their way. It may take work. It may take a kind of work that we're not used to and that's even painful. It's hard work. That's all I mean.

HB: Okay, fair enough. Personally, I've always held you up as the epitome of tolerance because you've had a long and happy marriage to someone who openly disagrees with your views. In fact, if I remember correctly, you once dedicated a book to, *Kathleen, who doesn't believe a word of it*.

So it seems to me that you have a very good perspective on the whole business—intellectually, academically and personally.

One final question: is there anything that we haven't talked about with respect to Platonism and its potential for world domination that we should have? Have we left anything out?

JB: I'm sure we've left a million things out, but life is short.

HB: Well, thanks very much, Jim. I had a wonderful time, as expected. It was a lot of fun.

JB: It's been an enormous pleasure for me.

Questions for Discussion:

1. Are you surprised to hear that specialists in "mainstream metaphysics and epistemology" are reluctant to consider real-world scientific examples? Why do you think this is?

2. Is Howard being too hard on Jim's suggestion of "being a team player"? Is there a danger in too many academics being focused on the same avenues? If so, what could and should be done about it?

Continuing the Conversation

Readers interested in a more detailed treatment of some of the topics discussed in this conversation are referred to Jim's books *Platonism, Naturalism, and Mathematical Knowledge*; *Thought Experiments in Philosophy, Science, and the Arts* and *The Laboratory of the Mind: Thought Experiments in the Natural Sciences*.

Defined By Relationship

A conversation with Charles Foster

Introduction
At the Heart

It took a fair amount of studied reflection to get the right sense of where, precisely, to place Charles Foster in the Ideas Roadshow universe. He holds a position on the law faculty at the University of Oxford and has written many legal books and articles on medical law. And yet he didn't seem quite right to be included in our Law collection.

He is a fervent environmentalist who wrote the New York Times Bestseller *Being a Beast*, captivatingly relating his pioneering experiences of temporarily living like a badger, otter, fox, deer and swift in a quixotic attempt to cross the human-animal divide. And yet he didn't fit our collection on The Environment either.

He is a Fellow of the Royal Geographical Society and Linnean Society, who has penned travelogues of numerous exotic locales and their societies, but it struck me as a decided stretch to put him in our Anthropology & Sociology collection.

Eventually, I opted to officially place him in one of our two Philosophy collections, despite the fact that he is not, by and large, officially regarded as a philosopher. But that, to my mind, is where he belongs: not so much because he is an unquestionably erudite fellow who can appropriately throw words like "ontological" and "epistemological" around with ease while penetratingly invoking key intellectual precedents from the likes of Aristotle and Aquinas, nor even because he is an acknowledged authority on medical and biological ethics, a universally-recognized domain of contemporary professional philosophy, but simply because it is unequivocally clear to me that Charles Foster simply *thinks* like a philosopher.

How else *but* a philosopher, I ask, would you appropriately describe someone who says something like this:

> "When I go into a wood I don't see a tree, except for a fraction of a second. And when I start describing that tree to myself, what I'm describing is **Charles Foster's thoughts about the tree**; and that's disastrous for a number reasons. If I want to know what that tree is actually like, I need to do better than that. If I need to relate to that tree, which presupposes that I know something accurately about it, I need to do better than that.
>
> "So it seems to me that we are in an epistemological crisis, and that lots of our neuroses boil down to the fact that we don't know enough about this world that we mooch through. And therefore we can't expect to feel at home in it—we can't expect to have our ethical attitudes towards the world calibrated remotely right.
>
> "We need to know more about everything in order to know where we are in relation to everything else; and therefore what should determine the ethics of our relationship to everything."

Many people, of course, like to invoke the importance of "relationships". It is the sort of vague, touchy-feely word that has a tendency to send sceptical people like me running headlong for the hills to avoid its many overconfident champions who inevitably feel inclined to follow-up their public avowals of the merits of "relating" with woolly pronouncements on how "everything is connected".

But Charles isn't like that. At all.

It's not that he shies away from adopting a significant number of decidedly eyebrow-raising views. He certainly doesn't. From *"the universe seems to be set up in such a way that it facilitates the ability of the organisms within it to have a communion with one another,"* to *"in order to know something, we have, Platonically, to undertake anamnesis, unforgetting; and children can help us to unforget things,"* not to mention a willingness to spend days of his life literally digging into the earth in a quest to establish some form of direct connection with other members of the animal world, it's safe to say that the world of Charles Foster is riddled with a good many perspectives that most of us, myself definitely included, would unhesitatingly label as "significantly out there".

He is certainly provocative. And iconoclastic. But he is not the slightest bit flaky. Which means that when Charles talks about the ethical implications of his theory of relationship, his ideas demand to be taken seriously.

> *"For me, relationship is absolutely everything. We can't begin to thrive unless we have good relationships with ourselves, with our human and nonhuman compatriots. If you try to say who Charles Foster is, you **have** to do that by defining him in terms of the nexus of relationships in which he exists. To take away my relationships I don't just become "a miserable, wretched, lonely creature", I actually evaporate: I cease to exist.*

> *"So to the question, **What is Charles Foster?** the correct answer is that he is the nexus of relationships in which he exists. And in order to understand my relationships and say where I am in the nexus, I have to first of all have an idea of who I am; and secondly, who the other things in that nexus are and how they are related to me and to each other. That's where it all comes from.*

> *"And since we relate—not just to ourselves and not just as humans, but also to everything else—that imposes a pretty crushing burden of inquiry on anyone who wants to feel at home in the world, who wants to **do the right thing** in the world.*

> *"That was the quest which drew Aristotle to be a passionate, natural historian; and I guess that's also why my butterfly mind has fluttered happily over the flowers over which it has."*

Philosophy, then. It simply has to be.

The Conversation

I. An Aristotelian Encounter
A mystery solved

HB: There's an interesting story connected to your case that I'd like to relate to you and then eventually, hopefully, come to a question—I sometimes have difficulties in coming to a question and this time I suspect will be even harder than most, but I'll try; hang in there.

So here's my story. I'm thinking about the next season's filming for Ideas Roadshow, and I say to myself, "*We should really beef up our law section; I should talk to some people who are expert in the law.*"

Now in many ways this is a particularly strange thing for me to be doing, given that I normally give lawyers a pretty wide berth, but business is business, so off I go looking to find appropriate people who are on the law faculty at reputable places who have written interesting and noteworthy things.

Along the way I turn to OUP's *Very Short Introduction* series and see your book on medical law. And I think, *Medical law—that could be interesting. That might be a good way to flesh out the law section. I haven't talked to anyone about that sort of thing.*

So I get the book and am quickly impressed by both the content and the writing style, while noting approvingly that you're a sufficiently credible person: a barrister who's a Fellow at Green Templeton College at the University of Oxford. All good. I contact you and you were gracious enough to agree to chat with me on camera.

A few weeks later I begin my preparations for our conversation. I go to your website to find out a little bit more about you and suddenly it all gets very strange. In addition to the sorts of things I was expecting—works on the legal and ethical issues of dementia, euthanasia, nursing, confidentiality and civil advocacy—I discover books on the biology of religious experiences, travelling through the desert on camels, a Pickwick Papers-like country tales of a hapless sportsman and tracking the ark of the covenant. And it just keeps getting stranger and stranger. It's not only that there's such a remarkable range of topics—which there clearly is—it's the sheer volume of them—prolific, an often very overused term, doesn't even begin to describe it. And to top it all of you're also, it seems, a qualified veterinary surgeon with a particular interest in veterinary acupuncture.

At this point all thoughts of focusing on medical law as a concrete way of tactically beefing up the Ideas Roadshow law collection have well and truly disappeared from my head. Instead, I'm actually beginning to wonder if you really exist or are simply an intriguing hoax perpetuated by some bored Oxford undergraduates—a secret society, perhaps, a collective euphemism for those who deliberately reject mainstream approaches to things?

I put down all the medical law stuff I have accumulated and start reading your latest book, *Being a Beast*, which I very much enjoy, but does, undeniably, appear to be written by the same individual who penned the other things I have dipped into. If there is, indeed, a hidden "Charles Foster Society" that is responsible for all of this, it is clearly one with a deliberately streamlined and highly focused writing style.

Your case begins to seriously intrigue me. I go down to the British Library to investigate more of your books, settling down with a more explicitly legal-type one on dignity (*Human Dignity in Bioethics and Law*). And then, finally, the fog begins to lift and it all starts making some sort of sense to me.

So here's my big thesis—I'm getting closer to an actual question now; I told you it was going to take me a while to come to it—these books are not, actually, as different as they appear at first glance. Or even, in fact, at second or third glance.

I seems to me that what you are is actually an Aristotelian. A genuine flesh and blood Aristotelian.

And by that I don't mean, some dusty Aristotelian scholar ensconced in a library somewhere working on yet another paper on the *Nicomachean Ethics* or something, or even somebody who simply has a broad-based love and appreciation of the natural world, like Aristotle did.

I mean somebody who is actually a kindred spirit of Aristotle, a genuine, modern-day Aristotle: someone who passionately and forthrightly investigates the nature of mankind and human flourishing in the context of the surrounding natural world.

So I have two questions, finally. The first question is, "*Is that right? Would you call yourself a died-in-the-wool Aristotelian?*" And my second is, "*If so, when did that start for you? Of have you always been inclined in that direction for as long as you can remember?*"

CF: The questions are very flattering. Of course, I'm no Aristotle, but I share his concerns. I'm passionately interested in human thriving. And I think the main reason that I'm interested in human thriving is that I wonder whether or not I am thriving as much as I can myself. The way that I framed that answer tells you what a very insecure person I am.

HB: Well, "insecure" seems a bit over the top to me; I would just say, "modest and humble". But maybe you are. It's a pretty silly thing for me to be arguing with you about your level of insecurity, after all. You see, you really do have me all flummoxed. Anyway, sorry for the interruption. Please continue.

CF: The world seems to me to be a massively fascinating place and a massively complicated place; and all those fascinations and complexities need to be assimilated somehow into our own view of ourselves in order for us to live as comfortably and as flourishingly in the world as we can. If we neglect to pay proper attention to any one of those little things, we're potentially not sucking as much out of the marrow of life as we might: we're potentially missing some key which we need in order to unlock a mystery.

So I'm concerned that our relationship with ourselves, our relationship with the wider natural world, goes off half-cocked because we have overlooked something which we need to know in order to properly contextualize those relationships.

In the context of *Being a Beast*, we have at least five senses. Aquinas said that we have ten, and I think he's probably right. But even if we have five, we usually use only one of those senses—vision—which means that when we look out on a woodland we are only getting, at the very most, 20% of the data that we need in order to properly interpret that woodland.

If we go into any other department of human life, other than "big understanding", we would think that there was something worrying about basing our judgements on only 20%.

In fact it's worse than that, because vision and cognition are intimately related for various reasons which we might go on to discuss: our visual images of things become transmuted immediately into our thoughts about those things. So our view of the world becomes almost immediately self-referential and narcissistic.

When I go into a wood I don't see a tree, except for a fraction of a second. And when I start describing that tree to myself, what I'm describing is *Charles Foster's thoughts about the tree*; and that's disastrous for a number reasons. If I want to know what that tree is actually like, I need to do better than that. If I need to relate to that tree, which presupposes that I know something accurately about it, I need to do better than that.

So it seems to me that we are in an epistemological crisis, and that lots of our neuroses boil down to the fact that we don't know enough about this world that we mooch through. And therefore we can't expect to feel at home in it—we can't expect to have our ethical attitudes towards the world calibrated remotely right.

We need to know more about everything in order to know where we are in relation to everything else; and therefore what should determine the ethics of our relationship to everything.

HB: You make a leap that is, I have to say, quite unfamiliar to me between epistemology and ethics.

The epistemological part, the epistemological crisis you referred to earlier, I think I get. There's the whole question about how we can be certain that the information that we are receiving from our senses and somehow, mysteriously, is being processed by our brains—invoking bits of memory and various other neural connections and relying upon this thing we call "consciousness" on the way—actually really represents the object that we think we're seeing, the object as it somehow is—what philosophers like Kant referred to as the *Ding an sich*, I believe—which is not only essentially the full extent of my German vocabulary but a true sign that you have me deeply floundering, because I am typically the last person you might imagine who goes around quoting Kant at people.

At any rate, I believe I understand what you're saying there—that there is a potentially highly significant issue between what we believe we are seeing and the thing in itself, an issue that is exacerbated both by our inevitably ongoing self-conscious interference—that you penetratingly described a moment ago as "Charles Foster's thoughts about the tree" in contrast to "our direct perceptions of the tree"—but also by the fact that most of the time we don't even bother to properly use all of the senses that we *do* have available to us.

So I think I get all of that. I've had similar sorts of conversations with neuroscientists, say, who invariably try to assure me—often unsuccessfully, as it happens, but whatever—that they have many of the answers to this sort of thing figured out, or they will very shortly.

But what particularly intrigues me, and seems significantly different about your perspective, is that from there you make an intriguing sort of shift towards the ethical—which is what I was trying, rather clumsily, to bring out in my opening statement—and it is this ethical orientation tied to what we might call a "natural science" or even "philosophy of mind" approach that made me think of Aristotle.

In other words, you move from this time-worn epistemological issue of, *How do we know that the external world is really what it appears to be because everything we know and believe is necessarily mediated through our senses and consciousness* and then rather quickly link it, or perhaps I should say "embed it", in larger ethical questions of where humanity fits into the overall scheme of things (broadly defined) and how we can lead flourishing, or at least more flourishing, lives.

CF: For me, relationship is absolutely everything. We can't begin to thrive unless we have good relationships with ourselves, with our human and nonhuman compatriots. If you try to say who Charles Foster is, you *have* to do that by defining him in terms of the nexus of relationships in which he exists. To take away my relationships I don't just become "a miserable, wretched, lonely creature", I actually evaporate: I cease to exist.

So to the question, *What is Charles Foster?* the correct answer is that he *is* the nexus of relationships in which he exists. And in order to understand my relationships and say where I am in the nexus, I have to first of all have an idea of who I am; and secondly, who the other things in that nexus are and how they are related to me and to each other. That's where it all comes from.

And since we relate—not just to ourselves and not just as humans, but also to everything else—that imposes a pretty crushing burden of inquiry on anyone who wants to feel at home in the world, who wants to *do the right thing* in the world.

That was the quest which drew Aristotle to be a passionate, natural historian; and I guess that's also why my butterfly mind has fluttered happily over the flowers over which it has.

HB: Well, I'm glad you've confirmed the Aristotelian parallel I've been trying so hard to establish, at least. Or perhaps you are just being polite—you are British, after all.

Questions for Discussion:

1. What are Charles and Howard referring to, exactly, when they make a distinction between the information associated with an object that we perceive through our senses and the mental constructs or representations we make of that object? Further perspectives of this issue can be found in numerous Ideas Roadshow conversations with both philosophers and neuroscientists, such as Chapter 4 of **Plato's Heaven: A User's Guide** with philosopher James Robert Brown and Chapters 5-6 of **Minds and Machines** with neuroscientist Miguel Nicolelis.

2. Do you agree with Charles' claim that until we successfully navigate through our "epistemological crisis", we simply "can't expect to have our ethical attitudes towards the world calibrated remotely right"?

II. Studies in Empathy
And the lack thereof

HB: I'd like to go back in time, if I may, and explore aspects of your own personal evolution. You're obviously somebody who has long cared very deeply about the natural world around you. In *Being a Beast*, you refer to a long fixation with blackbirds, your determination to try to get into the mind of a blackbird and never quite managing to do so, but nonetheless being very resolute in your efforts for a prolonged period of time.

You also mention, with considerable contrition, your past experiences as a hunter, having killed numerous deer and other wildlife when you were younger.

And once again, this is all very mystifying to me, given that I've honestly never been the slightest bit motivated to either get in the mind of a blackbird or shoot a deer. So perhaps we can just start there.

CF: Well, to start with, it's probably worth saying what I think I was trying to do with respect to the blackbird.

HB: Sure.

CF: I grew up in an outer suburb of Sheffield in the North of England. We had a privet hedge around our garden and in one of those privet hedges there lived a blackbird. And that blackbird looked at me with its yellow eye with a black pupil, and I looked at the blackbird; and what I saw in its beautiful eye enraged and tantalized me, because it plainly knew something about that little suburban garden that I didn't know. I thought I knew it pretty well. And I wondered what it was, and how I could find out what it was. I tried everything I could to try to get inside the head of that blackbird.

I did the obvious things: I mapped the flight paths of all the blackbirds across the garden. I went round each day looking at the various blackbird nests. I tried some things that people might think were strange or perverted, but which would have been regarded as simply trite in any animistic culture anywhere in the world: I scraped a blackbird off the road, stuffed it and mounted it on a piece of string so that it circled as a natural mobile above my bed as I went to sleep. And when I went to sleep, I held a forminalized blackbird brain in my hand, hoping that some of the wisdom of this creature would sink into me as I slept and I'd be able to understand better what it was about. Of course I got nowhere.

But I have been tantalized ever since by the question, *What did that creature know of the world?* And as I have grown older, I've become tantalized by the question, *What do any of us know about the contents of the heads of anything?*

So, you're looking at me now, and I presume that you are seeing what I see myself: an overweight, balding, middle-aged man, wearing a scruffy grey jacket. But I have no real way of being sure that that's what you're seeing.

But I have been worried, as I guess we are all worried at some point, whether all my conversations, with even those I think I know best, are conversations at cross-purposes.

When I talk to my wife over dinner, are we really agreeing about the basics of the conversation? Do I really know anything at all about what makes my children tick?

These are the basic epistemological questions; uncertainty about those questions propels people into the insecurities which torment me—and into lots of extremely boring philosophical papers.

But inside the head of every one of us there is a universe, the exploration of which seems to me to be hugely more difficult and hugely more fascinating than the exploration of the most distant galaxies.

I love the landscapes of England, Scotland and Wales, but I was worried that that love was based on inadequate knowledge. I wanted to give my love a secure evidential basis. What a pompous thing to say.

HB: That's not pompous. Strange, surely. But not pompous.

CF: And one way of trying to reassure myself that the love was securely based, was to try to perceive them more accurately. And that involved an inquiry into what the creatures that know those landscapes more intimately perceive of them—or at least what those creatures that are more committed to the landscape, more necessarily immersed in the landscape, perceive of them.

HB: So that part I get. What I don't get is the hunting bit after that.

CF: The hunting bit was a perverted form of that same inquiry. So I wanted to get close to these creatures. And I have read that hunters in other cultures needed to have a real clairvoyant relationship with these creatures. And it is true that they do.

So I killed lots of animals. I'm now deeply ashamed of it. I think that the expression of that legitimate desire was an entirely inappropriate one, given the relationships between modern man and animals which now pertain.

That said, I think that the intimacy between a man and a deer, when that man looks at the deer through the telescopic sights of a rifle, is a more intimate one than the relationship between that man and the same deer when the man is looking at the deer through binoculars. And I speculate in *Being a Beast* about why that might be the case.

It may be the case that I feel closer to the deer that I'm about to kill because we genuinely share one thing between us: *We're both going to die*. There's not the same intensity of connection with something at which I'm just looking.

HB: I see. And at what point did you realize that this was inappropriate, that you had to stop doing this?

CF: There was no one epiphanic moment.

John Fowles, I believe, describes how he looks at the body of a wader that he's shot and makes a decision then that this is illegitimate. There was no moment like that for me. There was just an increasing discordance between this epistemological inquiry that I was undertaking and the crassness of killing something. I realized that this inquiry should be based on, and should generate, empathy.

And the business of killing something seemed increasingly to be an unempathic thing to do. It was doing bad stuff to me, as well as to the things that I killed.

HB: One of the reasons I'm asking you this question is not to try to make you feel bad.

CF: I feel bad enough without you probing me.

HB: It certainly looks that way. My motivation is from a somewhat different angle, one that you can perhaps appreciate.

I've never been a hunter, but I've heard and read stories from people who have been hunters, who speak of the prey that they are hunting with great respect, almost reverence. And it's clear that these are also people who are very much in love with the landscape and the environment. And this combination has always profoundly bemused me.

Perhaps the easiest way to explain my bemusement is to put things within a modern American political context. A stereotype of modern American politics is that your average die-hard Republican voter is a rural, climate-change denying hunter and your average die-hard Democrat voter is an urban, vegan, green-technology advocate.

So this is obviously a gross generalization, but on the whole it seems fairly clear to me at least there's something to it.

But here's my problem: according to what you're saying now, and what I've long experienced myself, albeit anecdotally, on the whole it's the hunters who care, viscerally and deeply, about the environment far more than the urban dwellers. I mean, have you *been* to New York City lately? It's effectively one big garbage dump. Walking the streets of Manhattan you're struck by the irony of it all: I mean, it's hard to think of a place where the natural environment is so obviously *not* an integral part of people's lives.

So that just doesn't make any sense to me. It should be the hunters, the people who are deeply engaged with the beauty of the natural world, who are most keen to ensure that it is protected. **They** should be the environmentalists. But they're not—most of the time it's the exact opposite.

So that was the motivation behind my recent line of questioning. I was trying to get into the head of what a hunter feels and does.

CF: I think everything bad is something which is basically good, twisted. And I think that's what you see in this macho, climate change-denying hunting culture. I think that is rotten to the core.

One of the reasons why, in my experience, you don't see amongst those people a respect for, or even reverence of, the natural world and instead you see quite the opposite—a swashbuckling contempt for it—it is because hunting is too easy.

If you're killing something by looking from 500 yards through a telescopic sight and pulling a trigger of a high-powered rifle, you are doing something dramatically different from what the bushmen of the Kalahari are doing. You don't have to understand much about the natural world. You certainly don't have to crawl on your belly through it and have the natural world seep into you, in order to do it.

So, lots of basic connections with the natural world have been broken by the very mechanics in modern hunting. And that enables a psychopathic lack of empathy to be the most obvious characteristic of modern hunting.

Questions for Discussion:

1. Why do you think Charles refers to his belief that he "wanted to give my love a secure evidential basis" as pompous? What do you think he means by that?

2. Is empathy innate? To what extent can it be fostered or encouraged? Discouraged?

III. Childhood
A brief digression

HB: I'm going to switch gears a little bit now and ask you a very specific yet different sort of question. In one of the earlier chapters of *Being A Beast*, when you're being a badger, you have your son with you. Was it difficult to convince your wife that your son should accompany you?

I know very little about you and I know even less about your wife. Clearly you're a very energetic fellow in all sorts of ways, and I'm guessing that your wife must be quite a special person too. But I just thought, *I can't imagine my wife saying to me, 'Sure, take our son with you to live like a badger for a while.'* But perhaps it wasn't very difficult for her.

CF: It wasn't difficult at all. My wife is my wife because she is prepared not only to tolerate, but even occasionally to celebrate what might be regarded as dangerous weirdnesses.

But also, what my son was doing in that Welsh wood was what all children do all the time naturally.

HB: Well, come on.

CF: When I grew up, we spent ages living in dens, crawling around. I sometimes think when I look at my own children playing, *Are humans natural bipeds?*

They crawl around, they have their palms flat on the ground, they have their noses working, unlike our pathetic, redundant noses.

So my son took this all entirely in his stride. If you were to ask him now, "*What did you make of it?*" He'll say, "*Yeah, it was great.*" But it's no different from what he spends the rest of his life doing.

It's worth saying, too, that for exactly those reasons—that closeness of the child to the natural world—my children have been my great teachers. They have forgotten so much less than we have forgotten in our understanding of the natural world.

I have a fairly romantic, prelapsarian view of childhood. And my epistemology is that in order to understand anything, in order to know something, we have, Platonically, to undertake *anamnesis*, unforgetting; and children can help us to unforget things.

So, what he was doing in the wood was simply being him, and he thought it was intense fun. My wife saw that he would be happy being him, and therefore raised no problems.

Another thing, which is related to this, is perhaps worth mentioning. When I talk about this book, one of the consistent questions is, "*Didn't he get ill?*"

To which the answer is, "*Of course not.*" The human immune system is designed for woods and marshes; they're not designed for central heating and air-conditioning.

That question betrays a really dangerous assumption about the way that human beings should be living. We are designed for woods. What we were doing in the wood was not an eccentric thing at all. What's eccentric is to walk down a shopping mall or to sit in this beautiful house talking as we are now talking. That is physiologically dangerous, that is the really perverted activity. If you want to be a normal human being, crawl around a wood, doing what we were doing.

HB: Are all of your children of that persuasion? I appreciate that you have a deep respect for childhood and that you look at them as our Platonic teachers who are well-placed to educate us. I appreciate, too, your comments about the human immune system and the fact that what you were doing in the wood with your son was closer to what evolution has prepared us for than going to the mall—which as far as I can see has no redeeming features associated with it whatsoever.

Your approach to domestic family life is certainly not mine, I must admit, but it strikes me as perfectly consistent and quite admirable in its own way.

But I can't help wondering whether all your children agree with your views—you have six of them, I understand, after all. Do some say things like, "*I'd much rather go to the mall. Dad's really weird*"?

CF: Well, our seven-year-old daughter is perhaps reacting against woods and worms at the moment. But I'm sure she'll come back.

Questions for Discussion:

1. What do you think that Charles is referring to, exactly, when he mentions anamnesis and a Platonic sense of forgetting? Those interested in more background on this topic are referred to Chapter 1 of **Plato's Heaven: A User's Guide** *with philosopher James Robert Brown.*

2. Do you agree or disagree with Charles' parenting style?

IV. Engagement

Consciousness, relationships and different perspectives

HB: I'd like to talk a little bit about this notion of consciousness and connectedness which you alluded to earlier, and which you've raised quite provocatively, I think, at the end of *Wired For God*.

I appreciate that the question of the biomechanics of religious experience, a sort-of modern-day William James-type of approach, is something that interests a lot of people these days: how do we look at the variety of religious experience within the prism of neurophysiology, with a bit of epistemology thrown in.

For me, however, the most interesting part came at the very end where you talk about consciousness, suggesting that perhaps things are more teleological than we might be led to believe.

You say words to the effect of, "*Isn't it interesting that consciousness doesn't seem to be giving us any evolutionary advantage. Maybe what's really going on, is that our universe is somehow motivated to produce as much consciousness as is possible.*"

Perhaps you could say a bit more about your thinking there.

CF: Well, up until fairly recently, we've not been very good at looking for consciousness in non-humans. And the better we get at looking for it, the more we find it: the universe seems to be a garden, which is very fertile for growing consciousness. It seems to have sprouted up wherever we can see it. Why should that be the case?

Well, nobody has ever been able to coherently suggest why consciousness should confer any selected advantage. You can see why things which we sometimes conflate with consciousness confer a selected advantage—like theory of mind. There is an obvious advantage in me being able to understand what you're thinking.

But consciousness—the sense of self? No. All that I can see consciousness is good for, is relationship.

Of course, relationship itself, insofar as it generates community, has a selective advantage. But relationship per se is something that is Darwinially neutral.

So the universe seems to be set up in such a way that it facilitates, for reasons which confer no selective advantage, the ability of the organisms within it to have a communion with one another. I think that's very exciting. And the fact that is the case has all sorts of ethical corollaries for me.

HB: So I'd like to definitely explore those in more detail. But before I do, I have two quick questions to ask you.

The first is that it seems to me that one implication of this notion that there's far more in Heaven and Earth, consciousness-wise, than has been dreamt of in our philosophy, is that significantly greater numbers of lifeforms around us have at least some form of consciousness than we've hitherto recognized. Is that right?

CF: Yes.

HB: OK, good. My second question has to do with this notion of "the universe". Perhaps I'm just being a stickler here, and this may well be my physics background talking, but I can't help but wonder once you start invoking the notion of "the universe" that there's some larger principle of some sort that you're invoking, rather than simply saying, *"It looks like this is the way things happen to be on our little planet."*

Again, perhaps I'm getting carried away here, but might it be appropriate to conclude that you are suggesting, albeit somewhat inchoately and roughly, some sort of "cosmic relationship principle" where relationships are the key things and consciousness is a means to relationships and that extends throughout the universe and thus naturally encompasses what's happening here, or are you saying something much more specific like, *"Well, this seems to be what's happening around us on Earth and this is my speculative supposition as to why that might be the case."*

CF: I have no idea about anything that goes on outside of the Earth. I can see no reason in principle to suppose that the relationship-facilitating conditions on Earth wouldn't be replicated anywhere else, but on the other hand I can give you no reason to suppose that they would be.

HB: Fair enough. So let's return to Earth and to this notion of plethora of consciousness. And let me try to atone for my metaphysical universal speculations by getting extremely concrete.

As you noticed when you arrived here a short time ago, we have a dog. And one of the things that I've often remarked upon is the complete absurdity of the Cartesian view of animals—and dogs in particular—as automata: this notion that they don't have any awareness or thoughts or feelings or consciousness.

CF: No dog-owner believes that.

HB: It's simply inconceivable. All you have to do is just get a dog and you'll be immediately confronted with this overwhelmingly obvious fact.

But the legacy of this view seems to me to have been quite widespread and quite pernicious, extending well beyond dogs. Somehow, many otherwise intelligent people seem to have convinced themselves, by fiat, that no other life form other than humans has consciousness.

That's been a longstanding conviction in not only traditional religious spheres, but also scientific ones. But my sense is that our contemporary scientific understanding is finally evolving here, that with each passing decade there's an increased appreciation of more and more species that have some level of self-awareness. Would you say that that's fair?

CF: Absolutely right.

HB: Okay. So I naturally want to get to the associated ethical aspects of this, but before I do, I'd like to pose the fairly obvious question of limits when it comes to consciousness: Where, reasonably, might we draw the line? How might we draw the line?

Clearly we have it—well, most people, anyway. Equally clearly dogs have it. I'm not at all sure about blackbirds, but quite possibly. Amoebas seem a bit of a stretch to me, but perhaps that's just a sign of my closed-mindedness. Where should we draw the line? Is it even possible to draw the line?

CF: That's an empirical question to which I have no satisfactory answer. I can't see any reason in principle why panpsychism—the notion that everything is imbued with a soul of some sort, consciousness of some sort—shouldn't be true. It's not my own personal belief, as it happens. I expect that the line is to be drawn way beyond the point when you attribute consciousness to stones. Where it's to be drawn, exactly, I don't know.

I'm not sure that, for ethical purposes, whether something is conscious or not is the determining factor—but maybe that's something that we'll get to.

HB: Well, perhaps we should go there now and start talking about how these relationships have informed your ethical view of the world and how they perhaps should also inform other people's ethical views of the world.

CF: Okay. Well, I've said that relationships, to me, are everything. They are foundational to our definition of ourselves: *Charles Foster is the nexus of relationships in which he exists.*

And since I've said that consciousness is something that facilitates relationship, it would follow that the ethics, which I extract from my notion of relationality as essential to identity, is easier to apply to beings that have consciousness. That's a rather elaborate formulation.

It doesn't follow from that, though, that we don't have ethical obligations to things that don't have consciousness.

HB: Right.

CF: One reason, of course, is that when we do a bad thing to another thing, doing the bad thing hurts us just as much as it hurts the other thing—perhaps more.

Perhaps we'll talk about dignity in more detail later, but I talk in *Human Dignity in Bioethics and Law* about dignity being Janus-faced: how if I behave in a way that reduces the dignity of another creature, I might be reducing my own dignity a lot more than I'm reducing the dignity of that other creature.

So I do think that consciousness is pretty ubiquitous in the animate creatures that we treat in such a careless way. That conviction *does* increase the concern that I have for the way we treat them. But even if they didn't have consciousness, I would still be concerned about the ethics of maltreating them.

HB: Which also brings us back to a sense of empathy, I think—"getting into the heads" of other lifeforms as it were.

For me, some of the most evocative, and often very depressing, aspects of *Being a Beast* was when you would describe how different animals have had to adjust their behaviour due to man's encroachment on their environment, or detail how, given their advanced olfactory or hearing abilities, how smells or noises which are mere inconvenient disturbances to us might actually be very disruptive to them.

CF: Right.

HB: Which is all to reinforce your point that, from an ethical perspective, we don't even have to bring consciousness into play.

CF: No.

HB: As you express so vividly in *Being a Beast*, we can look at what we are doing to the lives of other animals, look at things from their perspective, quite independent from the question of to what extent they are, or are not, conscious.

CF: That's right. Even if a fox is only sensate and not conscious, the things which modern life does to our urban foxes are obscene. We force our urban foxes to be subjected to noises, which, for a fox, would be like us trying to sleep next to a jet engine. We have radically altered their sensual world, which is deeply regrettable, quite independent of whether or not consciousness is a part of their "ontological package".

HB: What's interesting to me is that this is something that I think is more accessible to people than they might appreciate.

I can imagine that many might think, *Well, how could we ever really know what might be impinging itself upon a fox or upon a badger or upon an otter?. That's just impossible to know.*

And you effectively throw a rock against that entire edifice and say, "*No, actually, you* **can** *have some sense of it.*"

And the key word is "some", of course. Nobody is saying that you can have a complete, comprehensive, picture of life from another animal's perspective, but there is—at least for me—a surprising amount that you can do, along the way getting a much better sense of yourself, your own abilities, and your own limitations.

Moreover, the very act of doing so helps give us a deeper sense of the world around us and our place within it. Well, that's my sense at any rate.

Are you finding that what I'm describing is a typical sort of reaction that people have after reading *Being a Beast*? Are people coming up to you and saying, "*Gosh, I'd never dreamed that I would ever be able to imagine what animals around me are feeling—thank you so much for giving me that perspective.*"

Or do most reactions tend to be more restrained and sceptical?

CF: No, I'm finding that people are almost always sympathetic rather than dismissive. I'm finding that people almost always recognize that they are more or less disastrously dislocated from the natural world, that they are missing something in terms of their ordinary urban lives by failing to be connected to the natural world, and are glad to know that there are fairly easy ways to reconnect: you can just drop six feet to the ground in your local park and smell the ground—something that you'd normally never do—feel it under your palms.

When we grew up, as human beings, on the plains of East Africa, we hoisted almost all our sensory receptors six feet above the ground. And we immediately had big vistas: we immediately saw the connection between things which had previously been invisible to us; and we immediately became beings who could understand in some ways, the ways of the wildebeest wandering better than the wildebeest did themselves.

But it came at a tremendous cost. Our vision became wedded, as we were saying earlier, to our cognition. And now we live almost entirely in our heads: we are woefully unsensual creatures.

But there's a way back. You *can* drop again—that six feet—and drop down the 20 million years as you do it, to the time when badgers and humans shared a common ancestor.

Or learn from your children who are doing that all the time. And you will have a literal sensory renaissance by doing that.

HB: And at the very great risk of sounding far too cognitive-focused and unsensual, the pathway you are offering here seems to be linked to modern notions of neuroplasticity as well.

You write about how by behaving differently, you begin to feel all of your own sensory capacities "coming alive", as it were. Which, I think, is very hopeful in many ways.

One might naively think, "Well, millions of years of evolution have run their course and there's nothing we can do, save indulging in virtual reality or whatever."

But it seems to me that you're saying that it's possible on an individual level to harness the brain's inherent flexibility to capitalize on often-dormant abilities through deliberately and explicitly changing our behaviour.

CF: Right. Everything we do produces physical changes in our brain and produces new neuronal connections. So, by using your nose in a way that you didn't use it before, you are rewiring your brain in a way which is going to be good for you—because your nose and your nasal cortex are *meant* to be used.

But I don't want to overdo the neuroplasticity business. I think a much more important part of what I was doing was simply learning to pay attention to things which we normally pay no attention to. And paying attention is a tremendously difficult thing to learn to do. I sit for about 35 minutes each day, cross-legged, with my eyes closed, paying attention to my breath or counting mentally 1 to 9 and back again. I've been doing it for years; and I have learned that you *can* learn to focus on the numbers 1–9. But it's a tremendously difficult thing to do.

And similarly, the practice in paying attention to your olfaction, which is normally ignored, is something that requires work and application to do. But it's a tremendously worthwhile effort.

HB: When you look around you, do you have a sense that, on the whole, most people are moving in a rather different direction from what you are recommending—which is to say, paying increasingly *less* attention to the world around them?

Notwithstanding the generally sympathetic and appreciative responses you've received from readers of *Being a Beast*, are we, on the whole as a species, paying less and less attention to the world around us—so much so, in fact, that there might be a point when there's no turning back?

CF: I oscillate between optimism and pessimism. Yes, I'm distressed and worried about our "goldfish bowl" attention span, but I also know from my own experience that there *is* a way back, and it's not a hard way back.

HB: Have you been able to influence and convert other people around you in your own nexus of relationships? Not to the extent, obviously, of pursuing some of the adventures that you've pursued, but this idea that people can become more in touch with the natural world than they have before. They can notice more things. There can be a greater sense of awareness. Are there significant numbers of people you've encountered who say things like, "You've inspired me to do things differently. I'm keen to try paying more attention to the world around me in a reasonably concrete way."?

In other words, I'm trying to determine to what extent your feelings of optimism are reasonably well-founded.

CF: Well, I say these things a lot and some people—quite a lot of people, actually—have said, *"Yeah, I see the sense of that. I'll have a go."*

Questions for Discussion:

1. Do you agree with Charles' position that "nobody has ever been able to coherently suggest why consciousness should confer any selected advantage"? How might those who disagree to him respond to this claim?

2. Are our sensory capacities in some way "in competition with" our cognitive capacities? Is it possible to imagine improving both of them simultaneously?

3. Has this chapter motivated you to in some way change your behaviour in order to pay attention to things that are normally unheeded?

V. Dignity

An overarching principle

HB: I'd like to talk in more detail about dignity and your use of it not only as a guiding personal ethical principle, but also more generally, in terms of concrete legal applications.

I found your book *Human Dignity in Bioethics and Law* to be particularly thought-provoking because you are able to point to a clear prescription for action, as opposed to simply saying, "*Of course we should pay more attention to dignity,*" which is very much the usual sort of motherhood and apple pie thing that everybody says, but doesn't actually get us anywhere. You might even say that "dignity", in fact, has had some bad press.

CF: Right.

HB: But you were quite explicit that we *can*, actually, be quite explicit and use dignity in a very practical way not only as an ethical guide on our day-to-day life, but actually in the law. How did that come about for you? What led you to this position?

CF: The context of the dignity book is that it follows a book called *Choosing Life, Choosing Death*, with the subtitle: *The Tyranny of Autonomy in Medical Law and Ethics*. I think that subtitle probably says all that I need to say about my view of autonomy.

So having written that strident, polemical, tub-thumping book—which was a very easy book to write, because it's easy to knock down something, easy to say what something shouldn't be—I thought I should attempt the much more difficult exercise of saying what I thought the answer *should* be.

In medical ethics and law, the four principles of Beauchamp and Childress have been routinely taught: autonomy, beneficence, non-maleficence and justice, which has to do with people having a level playing field.

The basic contention in my dignity book is that these are all fine and good, but they are second-order principles which plainly have a deeper derivation.

For example: beneficence, which orders doctors, say, to do what's good. Well, how do you say what's good? What criteria do you apply?

Respect for autonomy is fine, but lots of questions are begged by that. Should I have respect for *all* expressions of autonomy? Plainly not: I shouldn't have respect for the expression of autonomy which sends a rapist autonomously out to rape a woman, et cetera, et cetera.

All of these principles, when I looked at them, plainly had a parent principle; and one would have thought that if you want nuanced answers to questions which go to the root of the human condition, you should go to the parent principle.

So I started looking for candidates. And the more I looked, the more obvious it seemed that, something of what the Greeks were describing as human dignity was the most likely candidate.

You've mentioned that it's had a bad press in the academy. Mostly it's got a bad press in our contemporary academy because it's seen as incurably theological, as having its roots in the Imago Dei. And since God is out of fashion, dignity has tended to fall out of fashion.

So the challenge in trying to "sell" an account of dignity as the foundational principle was to articulate an account which was a secular one, which didn't depend on the notion of the image of God. And for that I essentially have to go to Aristotle and invoke the notion of human flourishing.

I describe dignity as "objective human flourishing"—making the most of the cards which have been handed to you by circumstances. And crucial to this account is the relational context in which I say all human beings necessarily are.

It's hard to be dignified on your own. I find it hard to say that an Athonite hermit there in his cave is thriving as a human being;

and therefore, although I don't like to be pushed to the conclusion, *Is that a person acting with dignity?* Probably not. He's probably not making the most of those cards.

HB: One very telling example you gave at the beginning of the book, which was particularly striking to me because I was hard-pressed to imagine any other principle applying when I reflected upon it, was the notion of an affront to dignity caused by inappropriate action to somebody who had died.

You imagine how we could determine whether or not it would be right to take the ear of a corpse and use it for an ashtray, or be kicking around a skull? And to our immediate, instinctual response that doing something like that would be an egregious affront to the dignity of the dead person, we are then forced to examine what, in fact, that means. After all, the person is dead: how can he have dignity? And from there we can clearly determine that dignity is something that must be considered to be in some sense an ongoing part of being even after death insofar as infringing upon it would be an affront to close relations.

So there's that whole calculus that you invoke, but then there's also the question, as you alluded to earlier in our discussion, about the damage to dignity that is occurring to those who would be engaging in such obviously inappropriate behaviour.

I'm a big fan of using specific examples to point the way towards the need for larger principles, and I think this one works admirably. Because it's clear from this instance that none of the other criteria you referred to earlier—neither non-maleficence nor beneficence nor justice nor autonomy—would allow you to determine the moral—and consequently potentially legal—inappropriateness of such an act.

CF: Right. Well, let me give you what I think are some more trenchant examples which make the same point.

Imagine a woman in permanent vegetative state. The consultant in charge says to the medical students, *"Come and practice your rectal and vaginal examinations on this woman."* The autonomy of the woman is not affected: her cortex is wiped out. It's difficult to say that she has any autonomy. You might say that, "*Had she had known that was going to happen, she would probably have objected to it.*" But as she is at the moment, her autonomy doesn't have anything to say.

What about "the good"? Our guts say that there is something bad going on here, but how do we *describe* that badness? You might justify what is being good in a utilitarian way saying something like, "*Future people will be helped by these medical students honing their skills.*" But although that's an argument for doing this examination, it's not an argument which helps you justify your instinct that there is something seriously bad about this. Similar comments apply to non-maleficence; and the notion of justice doesn't really come into it either.

Another example: a girl is seriously brain damaged. She's in the emergency department of a hospital. She's lying completely naked, uncovered on a trolley. Youths in the waiting room are very much enjoying the sight of her lying there naked. Is it wrong that she's lying there undraped? Yes. How do you describe the wrongness? It seems to me that that's impossible to do without reference to something which looks for the modern academy queasily lacked dignity.

So I don't think you can escape the notion of human dignity. Ultimately, even the dignity sceptics have to use a notion which is like dignity. One of the great dignity critics would have us put in place of dignity something like respect for persons. But again that seems to me to beg a *huge* number of questions. Why should I have respect for persons rather than respect for a brick? Who is "the person" for whom we should have respect? In order to define that person and to say what the content of the duties that we owe to that person are, we again have to come to something that looks like dignity, however we spin it.

HB: I'm struck by the way that you utilize a combination of logical rigour and the recognition of our instinctual response, that something just doesn't *feel* right. This basic, universal, conviction that, *We shouldn't be doing that*—even if we can't formally reject it in accordance with some established criteria, we somehow know that it is wrong.

I'm not saying, of course, that there's no need for some over-arching framework to structure our societies and our laws. As it happens, I'm personally a big believer in the power of logical structure and clearly establishing fundamental underlying principles, but it seems to me that if such principles don't somehow include, or at least correspond to, our gut feelings, we're going to have big problems.

CF: Right. I do think that we should listen carefully to our intuitions. They are vertiginously ancient and tell us quite a lot. I'm not in favour of legislating purely according to our intuitions—clearly, one can construct specific situations where our intuitions give answers which are plainly morally offensive. But dignity at least gives a way of talking about our intuitions in a way which allows us to examine their validity against some benchmark. And that's part of what I hope to achieve in this book.

HB: So how would you respond to the criticism—which you went to a considerable extent to proleptically combat, but which I'm guessing has nonetheless been levelled at you—that, "*Well, that's all well and good, Charles, but can you actually **do** anything with all of this? How can this be concretely applied and used as an effective principle of law?*" How would you respond to that?

CF: I think that simply giving this Aristotelian notion of dignity which I've just outlined doesn't help in itself. You need to have a fair amount of empirical evidence available as to what constitutes human thriving. And I think increasingly we are getting there.

I think, for example, it is plain that human beings do not thrive when they're on their own—I keep returning to this subject—and therefore things which facilitate relationship will be likely to increase thriving and therefore increase human dignity.

So, *dignity* facilitating things will be *relationship* facilitating things. There is, increasingly, a science of human happiness. There is a science of human relationship facilitation to which the law needs to listen. Law itself is offensive and intrusive unless it can be shown to produce human flourishing; and science can help us to know what generally constitutes human flourishing.

But also, simply to define dignity itself is not enough—even by reference to these broad criteria. You've got to have a framework for using it. And I propose in this book, a sort of quasi-utilitarian calculus.

When you're considering whether a transaction is ethically and therefore legally justified, you "add up" the total amount of dignity which flows in and out of it by assessing—in a sort of roughly Bayesian way, by reference to the proximity to the centre of the transaction—the amount of human flourishing which is affected by it. It's rather a convoluted idea—I do offer more detail in the book.

HB: Well, at the risk of being far too agreeable, I don't think it's particularly convoluted—complicated, perhaps, but not convoluted. And I would argue that to a certain extent these sorts of things have to be somewhat complex in order to be sufficiently rigorous. Of course I am not—most happily—a lawyer, and who knows what those guys think. I expect we will get to that one shortly. But for my part, I think it's worth pointing out two specific points.

First, I'm impressed by your constant advocacy of twinning grand normative or a priori principles with the empirical. You don't just say, "*This is what we should be doing according to this and that definition,*" but rather urge us to take into account recent scientific developments that are, in turn, based upon empirical studies and empirical evidence.

CF: Right.

HB: And the second point that I think should be emphasized is that you are hardly arguing that we should throw everything out that we've had before and start again from scratch.

In particular, you're not denying the relevance or potential applicability of these four criteria you spoke about earlier—autonomy, beneficence, non-maleficence and justice—but rather, as you say, seeking to ground them philosophically with an underlying principle—indeed in order to logically *strengthen* them.

CF: Absolutely. The four principles will, in most circumstances—if each of them is allowed to have a place in the conversation—produce a pretty good answer to whatever ethical conundrum you've got.

I raised the complaint that autonomy often seems to have too strident a voice in that conversation and that its voice needs to be heard alongside the other three, which is something that historically hasn't happened. But as a tool for teaching medical students, these four principles give you a very good start. It's a nice little thing to remember. But there are some situations where those four principles will not give you a remotely satisfactory answer; and where that is the case you have to go to the parent principle.

You mentioned the convergence of the empirical and the normative. It might be worth adding that I do think that when you're dealing with the most fundamental questions about human beings, it is unsurprising that the normative and the empirical are quite difficult to distinguish. And the fact that they're difficult to distinguish shouldn't be seen as a problem—it should be seen as a vindication that you got pretty close to the source.

I'm suspicious for all these reasons of the "is-ought gap", which forms such an important plank of analytic philosophy: the notion that you cannot derive what you ought to do from the way that the world is.

I think if you're doing your philosophy at a sufficiently fundamental level, there is no gap.

HB: The foreword to the dignity book was written by some appropriately well-established and influential fellow whose name I can't remember.

CF: Lord Justice Munby, as he then was.

HB: Right. And aside from all the typical glowing things he said about the book that anyone would expect a foreword-writer would do, he speculated to what extent we might be able to apply this dignity-based framework that you had developed even beyond bioethics and medical law and into other areas of societal import.

Which made me immediately think of topics like homelessness, which strikes me as one of the most obvious affronts to dignity imaginable, both on an individual level and also in terms of what it says about the very nature of our societies: that we're all quite inured to the idea that we will regularly encounter other human beings in our midst who are sleeping on sewer gratings.

Do you think that there's any way forward there? Might we be able to harness this essential notion of dignity more broadly, and more concretely, as a means to dramatically improve other aspects of our society? And, if so, do you have any specific ideas about how we might go forward and do that?

CF: I certainly agree with the idea. I'm not a very politically savvy person, and it seems to me that what you're suggesting is for this notion of dignity to be essentially used as a political rallying cry. I think it's potentially very potent as that.

"Dignity" is used in lots of international declarations and conventions, involving injunctions to lots of professionals about how they should treat their clients. By and large, the law has not had to say what the word "dignity" means in these conventions or other instruments. It's increasingly going to have to do so—these jurisprudential questions about what dignity has to say can't be dodged all that much longer.

Once the judges have said—hopefully agreeing with me—what dignity is going to mean, then perhaps dignity will have more of an edge with which to cut through some of the awful situations that you've talked about.

HB: And it also seems to me that there's an obvious and natural extension to be made here that naturally links up with many of the ideas you spoke about earlier.

Discussing the notion of dignity within the framework of bioethics and medical law, leads us to examine deeper issues of human interactions: human striving, human relationships, and so forth.

But very much in keeping with my Aristotelian portrayal of you, it seems completely appropriate to extend these ideas much wider to our relationships and interactions with non-human animals too.

CF: Spot on. First of all, in my account of dignity it is plainly the case that my dignity is diminished if I treat an animal in a bad way. It may very well be that it is possible to talk about the dignity of that animal in the same terms in which I talk about the dignity of humans: in terms of thriving interests of that animal. That animal plainly has some thriving interests, whether or not it has consciousness. Obviously, it has an interest in not suffering pain.

And to that extent, I would say that to cause pain to the animal is to affect its dignity in a way which should be proscribed.

So yes: while there's an awful lot of work to do in delineating just how this dignity theory might apply to non-humans, in principle, there's no reason why it shouldn't.

The difficulty will lie in being able to empirically determine what constitutes non-human thriving in order for this account to do all the work in a non-human sphere that it can in a human sphere.

I know pretty well what it means for a human being to thrive. There's a vast literature on it, and I know from my own experience. I can tell you a few things, I think, as can anyone, about what it means for a dolphin to thrive. But I can't at the moment, science being what it is, give you the same degree of explicit detail about what constitutes thriving for a dolphin. And unless and until I can do that, I can't apply all of my convictions about what dignity means to the dolphin situation.

HB: Right. I would imagine that there would be many different groups of people who would be very sympathetic to this entire approach, be they neuroscientists, zoologists, environmentalists, what have you. I would think that many would welcome the opportunity to use this as a way of more concretely joining forces or unifying across disciplinary boundaries in order to make progress.

CF: Yes. The people from whom I've had the most resistance are the lawyers; and I think the reason for that resistance is the fact that the word "dignity" appears as an entirely undefined placeholder in so many places; and lawyers look at that and say, "*Oh, because it's undefined, it's undefinable,*" which is of course, a non sequitur.

HB: Well, if you hang around lawyers so frequently—as you so inexplicably do—you're doubtless used to being bombarded with cascades of non sequiturs by now.

Again, I think it's worth highlighting that, for me at least, one very efficient way of shooting holes in these sorts of sceptical, hand-waving arguments (replete with non sequiturs or otherwise) is by giving concrete examples.

And with respect to the dignity of animals, you ask pointedly, after having discussed the obvious inappropriateness of a group of boys kicking a human skull around as a soccer ball, "*Well, what if that were an animal's skull?*"

And the answer—at least to me, and hopefully to most other people—is that it's still very much inappropriate: it's still offensive to the dignity of the animal and to the dignity of the boys.

And in this way, I think, we can move beyond all of these sorts of knee-jerk objections of, "*Well, we haven't defined all of our terms with the utmost precision and rigour and so we can't say anything at all.*"

Which brings up the obvious question that notwithstanding your obvious ability to convince *me* that there's quite a bit to your approach, what has the general reaction been from others—particularly all those dreaded lawyers? How sanguine are you about the eventual implementation of these sorts of ideas within our contemporary legal world?

CF: Well, it's had a probably sympathetic reception. Most people agree with you and me, at least to some extent. It's difficult to analyze, for example, the vaginal examination on the woman in a persistent vegetative state in a way that doesn't somehow involve the concept of dignity.

People are troubled by examples like that. They're looking around for something to fill the gap. There is this deep queasiness about the word "dignity", which, as I've explained, I think involves a suspicion of theology at its root.

But my impression is that "dignity" is no longer the dirty word that it has been—not just because of my work, of course, many people are working on this. So I think that there's a grudging acceptance, even amongst lawyers, that however vague the notion of dignity intrinsically is, because it's there in the instruments, they're going to have to make something of it whether they like it or not. And *that* has propelled an interest in dignity which I think would be unforeseeable 10 years ago.

Questions for Discussion:

1. Are you convinced by Charles' view that scepticism towards dignity is often the result of a perceived theological association? Might there be other reasons for a reticence to embrace dignity-based arguments by some members of the legal community?

2. How might our perceptions of dignity vary from one society to another? What, if anything, does this imply for the appropriateness or utility of using dignity-based approaches in our legal systems?

3. To what extent is dignity integrally associated with a well-functioning democracy? Readers interested in additional perspectives on this topic are referred to Chapter 9 of **Democratic Lessons: What the Greeks Can Teach Us** *with classicist and political scientist Josiah Ober and Chapter 6 of* **Democracy: Clarifying the Muddle** *with political theorist John Dunn.*

VI. Creating Impact
Changing hearts and minds

HB: Let's talk a little bit about the sociology of the legal community. I'm not talking so much about you and your particular ideas and opinions, I'm really asking a more general question about process. How do, on the whole, specific views gain or lose currency? Does it happen because influential justices start explicitly invoking them in their decisions? Media attention? Academic legal papers? What are the key factors responsible for people starting to adopt particular legal practices and arguments over others?

CF: All of the points you just mentioned are important, but the two most important are what the judges say and what the statute law says. What is declared in a statute about the basic values of a society is hugely important; and for that reason all the things that go into the making of that statute—all the lobbying, all the journalistic pressure—is tremendously important.

But also, because the reading of judgments is so significant—a vital part of a legal education—what the judges say is massively important too.

HB: I have another, rather different sort of question. I'm not sure if it's worth bringing up, but I think I will.

In your book on human dignity that we've spoken about at some length, you rail against Kant quite a bit. Now in many ways, I'm quite sympathetic to the idea of objecting to fusty Prussians who think they've figured out everything there is to know about human reason and human understanding according to some big formal system that they've developed in their daily, identical walks around Königsberg for decades on end.

So there's that. But then the other day I had a conversation with Onora O'Neill, the famous Kantian scholar, and my sense was that the broad ethical principles she was invoking were in some ways not altogether different than yours.

In particular, she talks about the categorical imperative as a principle of, or perhaps mechanism for, universalism. She speaks of how Kantian views of autonomy are views of autonomy of reason rather than the reasoner, and by Kantian views of reason, what she means is Kant's notion of practical reason, which necessarily involves the supremacy of the categorical imperative, which in turn necessarily involves this idea of universalism and the notion that reasoned discourse can actually proceed by invoking principles that all people could in principle follow and agree with.

So her view, as I understand it, on the supremacy of the categorical imperative and what Kant means by autonomy, necessarily involves human relationships, history, culture, people getting together to have reasoned dialogue and so forth.

Now I'm not a philosopher nor do I pretend to be one, so maybe I'm missing something very essential here. But my point is that this doesn't strike me as very different than your emphasis on relationships. Clearly the focus here is on human relationships and isn't pushed back more generally to the animal world and so forth, but she definitely seems to have developed a worldview of the importance of human universalism and human relationships that were inspired by her interpretation of Kant.

So I'm a bit confused. Do you see my confusion?

CF: Well, my problem with Kant is that first of all, it is silly to think that human beings perceive by reason, or what he understands as reason. Plainly what we value in other human beings is not their ability to reason. Plainly, lots of things which are the ethical products of reason are unethical. Lots of the people to whom we have to apply our own ethical superstructures are people who it is plainly impossible to attribute reasoning to.

So Kant has absolutely nothing to say to the patient who is in a persistent vegetative state other than that she is not a human being. And that is very deeply problematic for me.

And it may be that at the root of this distaste for Kant is my acknowledgement that he doesn't deal sufficiently with the relationality, which is at the root of all my convictions about what human beings are, and therefore my convictions about the way that human beings act.

I haven't looked sufficiently hard at whether that is the case to be able to plead guilty to that conviction, but I suspect that there may be something in it.

HB: Well, I'm certainly not recommending that you make the effort to do so, and I suspect that my confusion is more the result of different levels of interpretation by different people taking us further and further away from original philosophical positions. Perhaps I shouldn't have brought it up after all. That's what happens when you have all of these different conversations in your head, you see—they sometimes leak out at the most inopportune moments.

At any rate, I must say, Charles, that I've found that talking with you was a fascinating and highly stimulating experience, much as I had expected. Is there anything that you'd like to add? Something you feel that we haven't touched on, perhaps?

CF: No, I enjoyed our conversation very much.

HB: So have I. I must say, you're really a remarkably impressive fellow. Do please keep doing what you're doing.

CF: You're very kind.

HB: Well, I'm not, as it happens, saying it to be kind. It's just that I find you a wonderful example of what very sadly seems to be a dying breed—the iconoclastic and independent-thinking Brit.

I'm doubtless romanticizing this, but my sense is that your soggy little island used to be chalk-filled with types like yourself: thoughtful, deeply original people who impressively went their own way and did their own thing, but these days this place seems much more like "America light" than anything else. Which is a real shame.

And there's the fact that you are really exceptionally prolific, producing all sorts of things all the time, which is also deeply impressive to me. Of course I don't pretend to agree with everything you say, but that's not the point, of course. The point is to be challenged, to be engaged, to encounter new and interesting perspectives. And through your breathtakingly large and varied writings, you certainly do that in abundance.

So please do keep going. Think of it as your patriotic duty.

CF: Thank you very much.

Questions for Discussion:

1. What do you think Howard means, exactly, by his comments: "I suspect that my confusion is more the result of different levels of interpretation by different people, taking us further and further away from original philosophical positions"? Do you agree or disagree with his position?

2. Do you think there's anything to Howard's assessment that the uniquely British intellectual tradition is somehow waning?

Continuing the Conversation

While several of Charles' books were highlighted during this conversation, two of them—*Being a Beast* and *Human Dignity in Bioethics and Law*—are of particular interest to this discussion. As mentioned at several points during this conversation, Charles is a particularly prolific author. Those interested in his views are thus recommended to visit his website, charlesfoster.co.uk which will doubtless be featuring at least one newly-released work on one of his many interests.

Philosophy of Brain

A conversation with Patricia Churchland

Introduction
Of Mice and Men

Most of us are what might be termed "crypto-dualists". We recognize that, deep down, we are all made up of a highly sophisticated interwoven mass of cells, genes and chemicals that are arranged according to nature's rigorous rules that years of research is steadily beginning to penetrate. We consistently applaud the latest advances in medical science, recognizing their obvious import to helping us live longer and healthier lives. But despite all of that, we stubbornly cling to the notion that all of this increasing awareness of how to combat illness and improve our health and welfare somehow doesn't apply to who we *really* are. It's not *us*, after all—just our bodies.

But once the focus turns to our brains, the earth begins to shift under our feet. It's one thing to coolly examine how our feet or kidneys are put together, but our brains seem, well, a different matter altogether. However readily we might reach for a painkiller when we have a headache or frantically reach for our first cup of coffee to get us going in the morning, most of us have a stubborn, unshakable conviction that our mental states are somehow fundamentally removed from their underlying biological makeup.

Except, of course, that they're not.

Renowned UC San Diego philosopher of science Patricia Churchland, has made a career out of embracing the underlying neurobiology of our brains head on.

For Pat, the notion that our desires, beliefs, memories and consciousness are manifestations of the underlying neuroanatomical states might be a difficult one to accept, but that doesn't make it any less untrue.

> *"We have to deal with the facts. If you damage the brain, you damage those functions associated with the brain."*

Straightforward? Anything but. Over 30 years ago, when Pat and her philosopher colleague husband Paul were mid-career academics at the University of Manitoba, their views on the philosophical importance of the biology of the brain went largely unheeded throughout the wider philosophical community.

One person who did pay attention to the young neuroscientific philosophers, however, was Francis Crick, the celebrated Nobel Prize-winning molecular biologist who was a co-discoverer of the structure of DNA.

> *"Paul and I were at the Institute for Advanced Study in Princeton for a year, and I was invited to a meeting at Johns Hopkins. So I went, and there was Francis Crick. I gave a talk essentially saying that philosophers have got to start paying attention to neuroscience, because if you want to understand the mind, you've got to understand the brain.*
>
> *"Francis almost fell of his chair, because he had been trying to get philosophers in Cambridge to talk to him about this, but they wouldn't. He thought this idea was terrific, and he was a big part of the reason why we ended up at UC San Diego. We all became close friends very quickly."*

It was not exactly smooth sailing from then on in, however, as many philosophers were deeply reluctant to blur the line between the physical and the mental. Just like the rest of us.

Her popular book, *Touching A Nerve,* begins with recounting an anecdote where one of her academic colleagues found himself wailing aloud at a conference, *"I hate the brain! I hate the brain!"*— tangibly demonstrating that no amount of education or professional experience will necessarily provide emotional bullet-proofing from accepting the brain's anatomical reign over how we behave and who we are.

But embracing our brain biology also has its upsides:

> "I think it is hard to come to terms with, but the other thing I tried to convey in the book was that, in a funny sort of way, it is also very liberating.
>
> "Realizing that your brain is a biological business and that it's not that different from a chimpanzee brain or even a rat brain—that they share very similar organizational principles, that they have emotions like fear, rage, and anxiety, just like we do, and that they're probably mediated by very similar neurochemicals—I think that allows for a kind of identification with the biological universe that can actually be pretty inspiring."

Not to mention awfully informative.

> "When we look at the circuitry for parent-offspring caring and bonding, we see that there is circuitry in the mother for her own safety, warmth, food, and well-being, and that circuitry just changes a little bit once she has offspring so that it's as though the other is actually a part of her.
>
> "We really see this in mammals. We see a change in genes that produces a change in circuitry in the subcortical structures, such that if the offspring makes a squealing sound, the mother feels pain. If the baby rat falls out of the nest and squeals, the mother feels pain. She is instantly motivated to do something."

I think that's the basic platform, and then with other small genetic changes the caring can expand. We know now that rats will care for others. We know that mice will take care of one another's babies too.

Moreover, looking at our brains in the appropriate biological context also helps us cut ourselves a little slack when we behave badly.

> "We're often too hard on ourselves. Sometimes we do a stupid thing when we're really tired: perhaps we blow up at somebody. But

understanding that biological organisms are sometimes like that makes it easier to apologize, forgive, make amends, and carry on."

But most significantly, of course, is the promise of what the future might bring. For those who regard the triumph of biological thinking and the consequent overt parallels with other members of the animal kingdom as yet further reason to bemoan the intellectual descent of man, consider this:

"There are several fundamental things we don't understand. And that's why it's often helpful to look at simple animals—fruit flies, slugs, mice—who really aren't all that simple, as it happens. But if we can figure out some of the basic principles from these animals, almost certainly evolution has conserved those principles and then elaborated upon them, so we can get closer in that way.

"And if we get closer, then we have a shot at understanding things like schizophrenia, autism, and so forth. That's huge. When you think that, over their lifetime, roughly one percent of the population will have had a brush, or more than brush, with schizophrenia, that's enormous. I do believe that we'll get there, but it's not easy."

Suddenly, the line between biology and psychology begins to vanish.

To everyone's benefit.

The Conversation

I. Playing with Brains
Dissecting brains and meeting Francis Crick

HB: You might think this is an exaggeration, but my personal belief is that in two or three hundred years from now, when historians look back at this time that we're in now, they will point to the development of neuroscience as the most significant thing that is happening. I don't think that anything else will even come close in terms of scientific development or even, broad brush, what's happening to humans more generally at this particular time.

PC: I think that's probably true. But it's hard to see, in a sensible way, even twenty years out. Francis Crick and I used to talk about this sort of thing. One day he said to me, *"You know, in science— and neuroscience in particular—you really can't see, in any meaningful way, beyond about five or ten years. That's about it."* I think he had come to that realization after many years of pondering how much they **couldn't** see in 1954.

HB: You have this wonderful example in your book when you compare the search for some sort of mechanized device for genetic encoding—what, of course, became DNA—against protein folding. People said, *"This is the easy problem and that's the hard one,"* and it wound up being exactly the opposite.

PC: It did. Francis was very fond of that example because he wanted to make the point that your intuitions are really informed by what you already believe. They can't very well be informed by the truth about the future that lives in Plato's heaven, because there is no such thing. It's all about your intuitions, and your intuitions are going to be very hedged.

HB: And based on the past, which may have nothing to do with what the future holds.

PC: Right. He liked to talk about the history of science in that way. I could never talk to Jim (James Watson, the other co-discoverer of DNA) about such things, but that was a big interest of Francis'.

HB: It must have been wonderful to interact with him.

PC: It was. Meeting him was an amazing experience. It was a funny. Paul and I were at the Institute for Advanced Study in Princeton for a year, and I was invited to a meeting at Johns Hopkins. So I went, and there was Francis Crick. I gave a talk basically saying that philosophers have got to start paying attention to neuroscience, because if you want to understand the mind, you've got to understand the brain.

HB: What year was this?

PC: That would have been about 1982. And Francis almost fell off his chair, because he had been trying to get neuroscientists in Cambridge to talk to him about this, but they wouldn't. He thought this idea was terrific and he was big part of the reason why we ended up at UC San Diego. We all became close friends very quickly.

HB: Let's back up a little bit. You and Paul have these unorthodox views about the relevance and importance of neuroscience to studying philosophy of mind. First of all, where did these ideas come from? Then tell me a little bit about the reaction your colleagues have had to your views.

PC: It's always kind of hard when you look into your own personal history and you wonder where things came from, but I think I was basically in philosophy because I really wanted to understand the nature of knowledge, consciousness, and decision-making. I thought that was what it was all about, except it turned out it wasn't. Instead it was all about words.

By the time we had jobs, in Winnipeg, we were both really very frustrated by the idea that philosophers thought they could learn something about the nature of these processes by talking about the words that are supposed to apply to them. In a great way, Winnipeg was very liberating, because they didn't expect too much from us. So we had freedom to do a lot and nobody thought it was desperately strange for me to say, *"You know, I really need to understand the anatomy of the brain, so I'm going to the medical school and I'm going to talk to the guys in the anatomy department and see if I can learn something."*

The people in the medical school were sort of low-key, but very smart. And instead of being snooty and saying, *"You have no business here,"* they said, *"This is wonderful. Of course you must understand the anatomy. Come and take all the neuroscience courses the medical students are taking and enjoy yourself."*

HB: Did you actually have to get your hands dirty?

PC: I did all the lab stuff; and the most monumental day for me was when we had finished looking at cells and neurons under microscopes and they wheeled in this big trolley and we all got our own human brain.

They came in these Tupperware pots full of formaldehyde. We wore gloves because we knew about these strange diseases, like kuru, that you might still pick up from a brain. I was disappointed that I had to wear gloves, because I wanted to hold it with my bare hands. Anyway, out came the brain and then we were instructed on how to properly dissect it. It was the most magical moment for me. I mean, this was *somebody!* Whoever it was had done marvellous things: maybe they had been a farmer or a pilot, and there was their brain in front of me. The idea that we could understand what made it possible for people to do those things was so absorbing to both me and Paul.

HB: Uh-huh. Did Paul take these courses too?

PC: He didn't actually.

HB: Because he's a weenie like me?

PC: No. That one of us did these courses was enough. We had two small kids, we were both teaching; and to be fair, I was willing to be a bit more of a slacker in my courses than he was. Because I was spending so much time at the medical school I sometimes had to teach with very little preparation.

HB: Well, you were busy holding brains in your hands. You had things to do. So Paul has never held a brain in his hands?

PC: Actually, one day I brought a brain home, which I wasn't supposed to do, but I wanted him to see it.

HB: Well, you're a loving wife. That's what loving wives do; they bring brains home to their husbands. Perhaps one day my wife will do the same for me. But I truly hope not.

PC: At the time, my son was four and my daughter was two. They're both neuroscientists now.

HB: And what was their reaction to the whole experience?

PC: They could see that we both thought this was terribly exciting and beautiful, and impressive. But they also thought the smell was pretty bad.

HB: Quite so. But they overcame that and went into neuroscience anyway.

PC: Yes, they did.
 The magical, wonderful thing about Winnipeg was that they let me do these things. If I had been at a really high-class place like, say, Harvard, I very much doubt that the medical school would have been quite so welcoming. I could be wrong, but I think that would be the

case. Certainly the philosophy department would have put much more pressure on me to publish, and that means to publish mainstream stuff; whereas, in Winnipeg, they said, *"Okay, if you think this is important, maybe it is."* It was a kind of freedom that was priceless. The dean of the faculty could have lowered the boom on me, but he never did. He always encouraged me.

Questions for Discussion:

1. To what extent does physically making contact with a human brain impact one's philosophical approach?

2. Do you agree with Pat that there's often more scope to do pioneering research at a less prestigious university than a famous one?

II. Neuropioneers
Ruffling philosophical feathers

HB: So both you and Paul continued in this way, perhaps not quite always so rigorously hands-on, as it were, but certainly oriented towards a biological perspective. You wrote *Neurophilosophy* and you both became strong proponents of the view that the brain causes the mind. What was the response from your colleagues in philosophy as you started to do more and more of this? I'm guessing that many did not follow your lead and enrol in neuroanatomy courses?

PC: They hated it. They hated it from the viscera all the way up. Of course not absolutely everyone hated it, but many people had the view that, even if there is no nonphysical soul, you still cannot ever explain psychological phenomena in neurophysiological terms because the gap is too great.

Amongst philosophers there was this idea of what they called "the autonomy of psychology". What that meant was that you can think of cognition and all that fancy, high-function stuff as software running on the hardware. Now, if you want to understand, say, a word-processing program, you're not going to pay attention to the hardware—so the argument ran—so why should we pay any attention to the brain? You're wasting your time. It's very charming. It's nice that you like it and all of that, but ultimately it's a waste of time.

Interestingly, this idea is still pervasive, especially in the United States. For example, Colin McGinn, the British philosopher, published a review of *Touching a Nerve* in the *New York Review of Books*, and he hated everything in it. But in particular he reaffirms this idea that psychology is autonomous with respect to neuroscience.

HB: Does he just pronounce that?

PC: Yes.

HB: Does he give any justification for it?

PC: No. Well, what people did, by way of justification for that position, was kind of interesting. Part of the justification consisted in saying that, in the case of humans, our beliefs, desires, all of our cognition, is rife with linguistic stuff; that we are fundamentally and essentially linguistic creatures.

HB: So this is the Dan Dennett argument.

PC: Yes: Dan Dennett and Jerry Fodor. Jerry Fodor thinks that we are all born with a *language of thought*; and learning English, say, consists in translating from your *language of thought* into English. They think that cognition is inherently, intrinsically, and absolutely linguaform, whereas neurons could not possibly be linguaform, so how could that work?

HB: Here's my confusion, as somebody who makes no pretences of being in the field whatsoever. We're not talking about the 1870s or 1880s; we're talking about the 1970s and 1980s.

Even without any of the spectacular developments that have happened subsequently, in terms of diagnostic techniques, real-time brain scans, EEG, PET scans, fMRI, and so forth, people were still very well aware of the fact that if you had a pain, you take drugs and you feel better. If you take LSD, you hallucinate. There are some drugs that make you feel happy. There are some drugs that make you feel sad. The idea that we were already manipulating the hardware, resulting in different states of mind, was already pretty common knowledge, not to mention very prevalent in the public consciousness.

PC: It should have been.

HB: So the notion that these things are completely unrelated—sure, you might put up barriers somewhere and say, *"You can't describe everything this way,"*—but the idea that these are completely autonomous regions, strikes me as just so counter to our experience. That's what confuses me.

PC: It was bizarre, but I've tried to understand it. If you go back to the 19th century there was Helmholtz, who understood very well that events in the brain were really all about psychological phenomena and proposed that behind, for example, recognition of a face, there had to be massive amounts of non-conscious processing.

Some of the English philosophers understood that as well, and they started a journal called *Mind*, which was supposed to be "experimental philosophy"; that's actually the term that they used. Well, what happened? What happened was psychology sort of branched off and then there was logic.

You'll remember that logic really got off the ground with Peano and his axioms for arithmetic in the 19th century. In a way, what became the most powerful intellectual movement in England, and to some degree elsewhere, was formal logic. All of a sudden this thing which had been stuck in the Aristotelian framework for thousands of years—all of a sudden we had propositional calculus and quantificational calculus. You could do all these amazing things; and then there was the Gödel result. It was the most exciting thing going.

HB: All those guys in Cambridge with their analytic philosophy.

PC: That's right. It was all about logic; and then people had this idea that, of course, reasoning was really about doing this: it's about going through all of these procedures.

At about the same time we had Chomsky beginning to think about language, and he thought about language not as a biologist, nor as a psychologist, but as a mathematician. He thought of it in terms of following certain algorithms. He proposed, as you know, that there was the semantic part and the syntactic part, which was all about algorithms. How did they get together? Well, somehow.

This sent philosophy between this love for logic—and God knows I have that love too, because it's such a powerful, beautiful machine—and this idea that it's actually going to help us understand psychology. But it did not.

That's a historical guess. I'm not a historian, so I don't really know.

HB: But you're speculating, and that's certainly welcome.

The whole thing strikes me as very analogous, if not actually equivalent, to, a computer-science way of looking at the world: the software/hardware distinction you referred to earlier, formal systems, rigorous logic principles. It's almost as if the ideas is that you're somehow programming through language, or maybe a meta-language, but those are the tools that people were starting to bring to bear.

PC: One of the psychologists who was very important, and who was very close to Jerry Fodor, was a Canadian named Zenon Pylyshyn. It was his absolute, firm, unshakable conviction that all of cognition was essentially symbol processing. I used to say to him, *"How can that be the case for pain? How can that be the case for visual perception? How can that possibly be?"* He would say, *"Well, we start with beliefs, and desires, and problem solving, and then you'll see."*

So the idea was that it was a program, but I think, in retrospect, as you rightly say, as we see it now, it was like thinking that mice come into existence by spontaneous generation. Why would you ever think such a thing?

HB: It certainly seems to me to be a very curious assumption.

PC: It's very strange and it's still very pervasive within philosophy in America. As I said, it's changing a lot in England.

Paul and I were just total outsiders when it came to all that. We were just wasting our time as far as they were concerned. They thought neuroscience was never going to have anything to say about the nature of cognition, while our view was, *How can it do anything but?*

Questions for Discussion:

1. How, if at all, do you think that recognizing a linguistic capacity in other animals would influence the "language of thought" argument described in this chapter?

2. What role might dualistic views of the soul have had on the scientific development of how humans think?

III. Sociological Fault Lines
Mind vs. brain

HB: When did it start to change? When did you start getting some traction? After all, the world is much different now. There are still people on various sides of the divide, I suppose, and I want to explore that a little further within psychology. But the situation certainly seems to me to be very different now.

PC: The situation is very different and I think that is owed to the great explosion of data in neuroscience and people coming to realize that they could actually learn a lot about the nature of knowledge.

For example, knowledge consolidation: people like Allan Hobson were discovering that information is consolidated during deep sleep. This is not a process that's like going through an algorithm and making rational decisions: this is just your biology doing stuff while you're in deep sleep. That's why, if you've had a head injury and you can't remember recent events, you can still remember events in the more distant past. Furthermore, the idea that if the hippocampal structures are damaged, you can't learn anything new, is absolutely amazing.

Then I think the discovery with both H.M. and the Damasio patient, Boswell, provided philosophers with an interesting example. John Locke, and a great many people since then, had said that an absolutely essential part of your self-understanding is your autobiographical memory: if you lose that, you're nothing. Not so, it seems. There was Boswell who had maybe one or two memories from his past and couldn't learn anything new, but I could play a game of checkers with him. Now, he can't talk about having met me five minutes ago because he can't remember that, but he'll comment on this or that, and he'll ask me if I'd like a drink of water.

HB: He has a well-established character.

PC: Yes: he has a sense of himself. Indeed, it's diminished, but it's not like he has fallen apart.
    This was a way of showing philosophers that these kinds of neural facts actually bear upon philosophical theses. You can't just analyze the concept of self, as Locke did, and say that it must involve autobiographical memory. Usually it does, but it doesn't always.

HB: One can certainly speculate that Locke and other people of that generation would have thought differently had they been living in our time and were privy to this information.

PC: Locke certainly would have. He did, after all, dissect brains with Thomas Willis. Locke would have said, "*Okay, I was wrong about that.*"

HB: This is another thing they don't tell you when you're an undergraduate: apparently there's an alarming tendency among philosophical types to plunge their hands into other human brains given half a chance. That's all shuffled under the rug. So you're participating in a great philosophical tradition it seems.

PC: I know! I discovered that later and I thought that was wonderful.

HB: I've had the opportunity to talk to a good number of people who fit loosely into the category of "cognitive science", some much closer to biology and others to psychology. Through those experiences, I've become more aware of the nature of that divide, and it does indeed seem to be a divide. There are people who are hardcore neuroscientists and they believe unequivocally and without any hesitation that there is no distinction between the brain and the mind. There's clearly a subjective aspect to the mind, but what we think as the mind is caused by the brain. Brain states are responsible for whatever feelings, desires, beliefs we have, however complicated that process may be. In fact, they invariably tend to use the word 'brain'.

And then you have people who are on the other side, as it were, who believe that there is something else there. They don't deny that the brain has some causal effect on mental states, but they typically insert other things. They say things like, *"The standard biological view is incomplete, and there must be some other aspects to things."* They shirk from looking at neurophysiological justifications or causes for actions. And they almost always use the word 'mind' instead of "brain" when they talk about these issues.

It's quite interesting to see what's happened to the field of psychology because almost all of these people are at least formally in psychology departments, although they may be cross-appointed to medical schools, or what have you, depending on their proclivities and attitudes.

From my perspective, it seems like this field is in rapid transition sociologically, as these fault lines are becoming better defined and more people are coming out on each separate side. Is that an accurate depiction of what's going on? How do you see the change in the fields of psychology and cognitive science?

PC: It's a big question. At the risk of oversimplifying a little bit, I basically do see it in much the same way that you do.

Within a psychology department, such as ours here at UCSD, there are some people who are really focused at the behavioural level and do brilliant work at that level—for example, Hal Pashler's work on attention. He is quite happy to stay at that level because there is still a lot of information that he can mine, but I don't think he sees it as understanding phenomena that are unrelated to the brain. I think he sees it as providing additional data and constraints for somebody like John Henderson who works on the neurobiology of attention. He sees it as a constraint for that kind of work.

HB: So he's adding extra information. But wouldn't he want to just go and look at an fMRI? Wouldn't he want to put some of his experimental subjects in one of these machines to see what's actually happening in the brain? It seems like a lot of these people just say, "No, I don't want to deal with that. I'm not an fMRI kind of person. There's too much of that stuff in the field. We should be doing more behavioural experiments."

PC: I don't know. I guess one's take on the sociology of this is going to depend on the particular people that you happen to meet. In the psychology department at UCSD there are people who do precisely that: they put people in the scanner and see what's going on.

Personally, I see the two sides coming closer together. One of the people whose work I track quite closely in the psychology department you might think of as a cognitive neurobiologist because he works on self-control, on the specific pathways in the prefrontal cortex and their connection to the reward system and other subcortical structures. I see the divide as being less pronounced than it was in, say, the 1980s.

HB: So the line between the two is getting fuzzier?

PC: It seems to me that that would be true of UCSD. On the other hand, I've met other psychologists who are more of the description that you gave: they want to say, *"I'm working on the mind and to understand that I need to know the behavioural parameters of—"* whatever it is they're interested in. But that seems to me to be rarer now.

HB: As you rightly say, logically the two attitudes are not at all mutually exclusive. The more behavioural evidence you have, the more that can be added to the great melting pot of knowledge. It's just that to me there's a big difference between saying, *"I am working on behavioural evidence as a means of furthering this investigation globally,"* as opposed to declaring, *"I am working on behavioural evidence, which is the only way to understand these things, and everyone else is wasting their time."*

PC: That's right. And there are still people who want to say that. I think this is still kind of a throwback to the idea that psychology is working on the software. Why would you take apart your computer if what you wanted to understand is why your email program isn't working? That's kind of the mindset.

But on the other hand, I think that is being chipped away by new discoveries. Think of Walter Mischel's marshmallow test: you tell a kid that you'll give them one marshmallow now, or four when you come back in a few minutes. It turned out that, when they tracked those kids over long periods of time, the ones that were impulsive differed in their career trajectories and lifestyles from the ones who had self-discipline. Those who showed self-restraint tended to go to college, get a job, have stable relationships, and didn't do drugs, statistically speaking; whereas, on average, those test subjects who lacked self-restraint performed lower on those measures.

Thirty years later they gathered as many of those original subjects as they could and they scanned them. They saw interesting differences between the two populations.

HB: What did they see, exactly?

PC: They saw interesting differences where you would expect to see them: the prefrontal cortex.

HB: That's the area that's responsible for executive planning and that sort of stuff, right?

PC: That's right. And other work has taken very young children and compared those who live in very stressful conditions with poor impulse control to those who live in normal conditions who have relatively good impulse control. When they scanned them it turns out that the stress has a definite impact on their pre-frontal cortexes.

People like Robert Sapolsky and others have shown that, at a micro level, chronically high levels of stress, high levels of stress hormones sloshing around in the brain, kill neurons, preferentially in the pre-frontal cortex. This is one of those wonderful examples where you can see the thread between a high level "mental" operation (self-discipline or the capacity to delay self-gratification) all the way down through the levels of the nervous system.

I think when graduate students, post-docs, and young faculty think about these things, they realize it doesn't make sense anymore to talk about "the autonomy of the mind".

HB: It's just putting up these ridiculous artificial barriers.

PC: Why would you do that? Why would you turn your back on information that is obviously useful? That's just dumb.

HB: Well, that's a fundamental thesis of *Touching a Nerve*, of course, and I'd like to talk about that more generally. But before we get there, I'd like to say something that is potentially provocative about the discipline of the philosophy of science and philosophy of mind in general.

Questions for Discussion:

1. Do you think that we'll ever be able to "read someone's personality" by looking at their brain scan?

2. Are there downsides to the rapid development of modern neuroscience? If so, how might they be dealt with in the future?

IV. Connecting Horizontally
Investigating "philosophy of mind"?

HB: So now it's time for me to be provocative, as promised/threatened.

I'll start with a famous quote from Richard Feynman. Apparently, when he was asked about the merits and the relevance of philosophers of physics, he said, "A philosopher of physics is to a physicist what an ornithologist is to a bird," which I take to mean something like, *they're doing what they're doing, but they have no influence whatsoever on the generation of the actual insights and understanding involved in the field.*

As you know, I had this rather singular experience of building a theoretical physics research institute from scratch some years ago. My attitude was that we should try hard to deliberately circumvent the many silly labels that spring up from time to time that might get in the way of legitimate knowledge generation.

Regardless of whether somebody currently hangs her hat in a philosophy, physics, computer science or mathematics department, it seemed appropriate to try to create an environment where she could be included in the research culture if what she had to say was of legitimate merit and import. Perhaps it was a bit Utopian—I was pretty young at the time, after all—but the general motivation was pretty basic and common-sensical, I think: to try to pare away arbitrary labels to involve as many appropriate people as possible in the overall research effort to increase the likelihood of success.

I don't want to get into whether it was actually successful or not—which is hardly for me to weigh in on anyway— but when I listen to you and I read your papers, much of this comes flooding back to me. More specifically, my view is that you are somebody who's contributing to this great pursuit of understanding the brain: how it functions, how, at some deep level, it causes, or at least triggers, different manifestations of human behaviour, and so on.

So that's all fine and good. But then why do so many philosophers who purport to be contributing to the same research effort feel the need to start throwing around terms like "philosophy of mind", which is a label that I don't even pretend to understand? What is it, exactly? Why does it exist? Aren't you just involved in this great, compelling field of cognitive science and we should just leave it at that? Why throw around grandiose-sounding phrases like "philosophy of mind" at all? Is there supposed to be something that philosophers contribute to this venture that your colleagues in neuroscience somehow don't or can't?

And before I let you answer, I'll tell you what a philosopher of physics tends to say to a physicist when faced with this exact question, which is something that has long irritated me (as well as, I think, a lot of other physicists). Typically, a philosopher of physics will say something like, *"Oh yes, the physicists work on their theories, but **we** work on trying to **understand** the theories."*

So if you're a theoretical physicist, you're naturally going to think to yourself, *"Hang on: you're telling me that if **I'm** working on developing **my** theory, I need **you** to be able to explain it to me? What nonsense!"*

Are "philosophers of mind" playing the same sort of games, or is there something actually objectively meaningful in that particular label?

PC: It's a very good question and one well worth pondering. Let me give you another quote from John Wheeler, which is even worse, if that's possible. He said, *"Here is my understanding of philosophers. They're like tin cans tied behind a car: they make a lot of noise; they don't serve any purpose; and they're always behind."*

But it's an interesting question. My feeling is that philosophers may not actually serve any particular purpose at this point, now that neuroscience has flowered to the degree that it has.

One thing I think may be useful to do—and this may be similar to philosophy of physics, or it may not be—by and large, whether you're in cognitive science, psychology, or neuroscience, you really have a very narrow, vertical take on what you're doing. You can expand a little bit, and if you're in the bathtub you might read a New Yorker article on some aspect of neuroscience that's way out of your field, but by and large, you have to go vertically. You have to spend a lot of time getting the experiments right, and set up properly, and so forth.

I feel that one of the things that I can do—and I think there are some other philosophers who do this too—is that after you've done all your experiments, you can tell me what your results are. I will understand them because I've put in enough time to try and make sense of things, and I can do this nice thing where I make horizontal connections. Sometimes that allows me to bring together, or to synthesize, in a way that you might not be able to do.

One response might be, *isn't that just journalism?* I think the answer is that a journalist probably can't spend most of her life studying and thinking about neuroscience, whereas I basically have.

HB: Well, you have to have enough depth to make these connections, which is what you're saying.

PC: Yes. Sure you could say that I'm just a highfalutin journalist, or "a cheerleader," as Colin McGinn says; but, actually, I think it does mean that I can pull things together in a way that can sometimes be useful.

HB: I didn't actually mean to be attacking you. In fact, I was trying to attack your entire discipline; I was actually making an exception for you.

PC: Well, they think I'm attacking them too and of course, to a degree, I am. I think there are lots of things that philosophers can do. For example, exploring the interface between neuroscience and the law can be very useful. Some philosophers are helping to keep the great books alive, and there is something to be said for that also. But I absolutely agree that there really isn't a separate field called "philosophy of mind" where you can achieve some progress.

One of the things that people ask me at Janelia Farm (a scientific research campus of the Howard Hughes Medical Institute) is very much like what you were asking. They say, *"We keep hearing from philosophers that they're going to save us from all these 'conceptual problems' that we have. Do you think that you're saving us from conceptual mistakes?"* And I say, *"You know, I really hate to criticize my colleagues, but I don't think so. I don't see these big mistakes being made."*

Here's one of the mistakes that neuroscientists apparently all make: they talk about the brain as falling asleep, or as remembering, or as seeing. The philosophers say, *"Tut-tut. It's not the brain that does those things; it's the person."* Well, fine, but we go on talking about that anyway and it's neither a very big nor a very interesting point.

Recently a philosopher said to me, *"You know, we're really saving neuroscientists from going off in many different bad directions by pointing this out to them."*

"Well, name one", I replied.

My own feeling is that philosophers would like it to be true that they're resolving all these conceptual tangles that scientists can't handle. But that's not really true.

Questions for Discussion:

1. *Should scientists study philosophy?*

2. *Was Einstein also a "philosopher of science"?*

V. Touching a Nerve
Spreading the message

HB: This brings up what, it seems to me, is a primary thesis of your book, Touching a Nerve: it's not enough to just believe something because it makes us feel good. It may be nice to believe in it. Sure, we all have fears and desires, and so forth. But when the stakes are sufficiently high—like, for example, if somebody is suffering from some illness or is diagnosed with a disease that requires treatment—it's not enough to just wish it away. In order to make genuine progress we actually have to roll up our sleeves and deal with things.

PC: We have to deal with the facts.

HB: Right. So this notion that the world is filled with both positive and negative things and we would all be better off if we acted more like grown ups—I'm simplifying a lot, but this is one central aspect of the thrust behind your book, it seems to me. It may make us feel uncomfortable to look at ourselves as just a brain or a lump of meat, and it may be confusing and difficult, but that's just the way it is and we'd be better off accepting that and moving forwards.

By analogy, it seems like when these philosophers say things like, *"There are some grand constructs out there. These neuroscientists are making a logical error because when somebody is sleeping there has to be a person, and therefore there is a mental state, and therefore that mental state has to be abstracted"*—it's almost like they're playing linguistic games.

PC: I think they are. I think it is kind of wishful thinking on their part. They want to think that they are useful, that they're helping the neuroscientists avoid conceptual errors. But I just don't see it.

HB: You start *Touching a Nerve* by demonstrating that this idea that the self is a manifestation of the brain, that we can map what we all feel to a neurophysiological state, is hard for everyone. As an example—again, it seems like I'm determined to beat up on philosophers here—you highlight an anecdote of this one philosopher who stood up, in a conference, and screamed, *"I hate the brain! I hate the brain!"* Then you speculate about what that might mean. But I have another question: who was that guy? Can you tell me?

PC: I don't think I should. Part of me would like to, but I think that it was such an embarrassingly stupid thing to say that I feel I just couldn't do that.

HB: That's probably best. But I guess the more substantive aspect of all this is that we have on display a sentiment that cuts across all sorts of lines. It cuts across educational levels, vocation, where you live in the world, your experiences.

It's a very difficult thing for people to come to terms with because it's particularly challenging to identify what we consider to be ourselves—this thinking human being with desires, beliefs, memories, and consciousness—it's very difficult to reduce that to the brain.

PC: I don't like to use the word "reduce" because people get very frightened by that word. But you're right that it's all a manifestation of the brain itself, as you said before. If you damage the brain, you damage those functions. I think it is hard to come to terms with, but the other thing I tried to convey in the book was that, in a funny sort of way, this is also very liberating.

I think that realizing that your brain is a biological business and that it's not that different from a chimpanzee brain or even a rat brain, that they share very similar organizational principles, that they have emotions like fear, rage, and anxiety just like we do, and that they're probably mediated by very similar neurochemicals—I think that allows for a kind of identification with the biological universe, which is actually kind of cool.

The other aspect of this is the recognition that sometimes we're too hard on ourselves. Sometimes we do a stupid thing when we're really tired: perhaps we blow up at somebody, say. Just understanding and appreciating that, in fact, biological organisms are like that, makes it easier to apologize, forgive, make amends, and carry on.

I think the same is true of certain kinds of changes in the brain. I was explaining before about my brother and how liberating it was for him to realize that there was a medical explanation for his poor impulse control and poor planning. Or take going through puberty. If ever there was an argument for saying that the mind is a product of the brain, surely it's going through puberty. All of sudden you've got these changes in hormone levels in the brain and you start finding things interesting that you used to find odious and you readily engage in certain behaviours which you couldn't imagine doing before. You start thinking about certain things obsessively. How else are estrogen and testosterone going to affect the mind except by affecting the brain? I think it is kind of liberating and makes you feel at home in the world in a certain sort of way.

HB: In terms of your motivation for writing this particular book, was it more to spread that particular message? Was it to apprise people of what's actually happening? Was it to paint a picture of some interesting developments and some of the fault lines? What were you trying to achieve?

PC: I think all of those things. I did particularly want to address the anxiety that people have in light of the realization that the brain is what it is. I did want to get across the idea that you don't have to wallow in the fearfulness of it, that there is something splendidly wonderful that you can behold by appreciating that you're this wonderful, biological organism. But I did also want to bring people in to show them where things are and where they aren't. There are lots of things that remain puzzling to us, and I wanted to convey that as well. All of those things seemed to be worth talking about.

I had written academic books before, books that were much more technical and were really meant for a slightly more narrow audience. I really felt motivated to spread my wings a little bit.

HB: What was the reaction generally? You mentioned the dismissive review in the *New York Review of Books* earlier by Colin McGinn, but what was the broader-based response from people both within the community and outside of it? Was there a sense that finally someone was saying these things to the general public or was the response largely negative? In short, what was the overall response and did it surprise you at all?

PC: I was surprised that the response was so overwhelmingly positive and that the people who were writing as more general reviewers, as opposed to as specialists, loved it. Abigail Zuger, who is an MD who often writes for the *New York Times*, loved it, and she wrote a super review that showed she obviously really understood it. Adam Gopnik also talked about it in *The New Yorker*. I was happy about that. And the specialist magazines like *Nature* and *Science* gave really nice reviews also.

On balance, I think it did quite well. And, on a more popular level, maybe one index is that I was on *The Colbert Report*.

HB: How was that?

PC: It totally threw me that I was asked at all. I was just flabbergasted. Of course I said, "Yes." It was so much fun. I'm not sure if you saw the clip—

HB: I did. I saw the public version, at least. Of course, I don't know what it was like behind the scenes.

PC: He doesn't talk to you in advance, so you really don't know what he's going to say. He came into the green room and he said, *"I'll be* *in character. Just remember that,"* and off he went. I found it to be really fun and enjoyable.

I think he hadn't heard the story of how prairie voles mate for life and how they have this special array of oxytocin receptors, which seems to be an important part of the explanation. It was great fun. I got a lot of emails after that and there was a huge spike in book sales.

I think it made people think a little bit about how a very complex bit of behaviour, bonding with a mate for life, has a very biological basis.

HB: Right. Well, what other basis could it have?

PC: Exactly.

HB: But again, these questions need to be put out there in the public consciousness. That's what I was really asking about in terms of response, because academic colleagues will do one thing, and people at *The New Yorker* might do something else. But I was wondering whether or not it was appreciated by, or resonated with, people who weren't specialists, who might think twice about this to get a sense of what is really going on.

PC: I got some emails from people in the South who said, *"I've been thinking that maybe something like this was true for a long time, but I didn't dare say anything. I couldn't believe it when you said it. I was so relieved."* I found that very interesting.

HB: That was another thing I wanted to ask you about in terms of response. Colbert was in character of course, and his character was extremely conservative. But it's not unreasonable to imagine that taking a predominantly biological perspective on human actions and behaviour might offend those with strong religious sensibilities. Did you experience that yourself?

PC: A little bit. I got maybe three or four emails like that. One of the things I learned from an anthropologist who studies religion is that a lot of people don't literally believe that sort of credo. If you ask them about what they really think happens after they die, they don't actually think that there is some little thing that comes out of their head and ascends to heaven. But it's something that they participate in as part of a community ideology.

HB: You highlight issues that have preoccupied people in different societies for thousands of years: if I die and I previously had a leg amputated, is that leg reunited with my body after I die? People have long known about the putrification of corpses and all of that, so there is a long history of these sorts of questions.

PC: And, of course, Buddhists have not really believed anything quite like that, by and large. A lot of Asians actually really resonated with that part of the book and with the idea that religion doesn't need to involve a deity who is divine and lives in paradise. It can just be a way of living life that makes sense in terms of community, decency, kindness, and so forth. That really is kind of the Buddhist and Confucian story, and there are billions of people whose religion is like that, rather than believing there's an old guy up there in the clouds.

Questions for Discussion:

1. Is there a way of logically reconciling contemporary neuroscience with the beliefs of standard monotheistic religions?

2. Do you agree that embracing our inherently physiological makeup can make us feel more connected to the surrounding biological world?

VI. Social Relevance

Explorations of morality through biology

HB: I want to talk about the social relevance of contemporary neural scientific awareness and how this applies to the average person.

You mentioned the law earlier. There are obvious aspects of ethics and morality as well. In your view, what is the resonance of all of this for people who go about their lives doing all sorts of interesting things that don't have any obvious overlap with neuroscience or cognitive science? Not just because they may find this interesting, but because they might think it's relevant on a societal level.

Here's an example of the sort of thing that I'm thinking about. If I'm somebody reading this, I might say *"Hang on, you were talking about people whose behaviour can be explained by neurophysiological means. When someone hits puberty, of course something is happening; hormones are raging in the brain. If you have a difficult day and you blow up at somebody, maybe there's a neurophysiological explanation. But doesn't this let people off the hook far too easily? No matter what people do they can say, 'It's not really me; it's actually my brain that's doing that.'"*

I can imagine that some people might think that's going too far, because you're allowing people to abdicate all responsibility for their actions and you're saying their actions are inevitable biochemical responses in the brain. How would you respond to that?

PC: I think that is an important thing to reflect on. My view is something like this. Socialization—and this is not only true of the human species, but others as well—involves certain parameters, certain rules and norms of behaviour. If you violate those norms you are pulled back in. You are pulled back in often by disapproval, or punishment, or what have you. If a young wolf, for example, fails to draw back when his playmate rolls over and exposes his throat, and the young wolf goes for the throat instead, the other wolves are instantly there and they chase him off. That's a very severe punishment for a wolf. I think that an important part of socialization is tuning up the reward system so that we can expect—not only as children, but also as adults—that if we violate the norms or the social practices in a way that hurts other people, there will be payback.

That's part of the reason why I think Stephen Morse and other jurists who think about the possible impact of neuroscience on the law are inclined to say that the impact may, at least at first, be fairly minimal, because criminal law is really about social safety. To a degree, it's also about retribution, but I'll get back to that later. What we're concerned with in criminal law is the question of whether the perpetrator is going to do it again. If you did something stupid, like release pigs from a pen while you were sleepwalking, that's potentially treatable to ensure you don't sleepwalk again. But if you were fully awake and planned a Ponzi scheme over the years, then we think that you are likely to do it again and we put you away. That's why I think the law is not going to change that much as a result of neuroscience.

Now, to a degree, retribution also figures into the law. That's because if those who are victimized by assault, or by Ponzi schemes or whatever, do not see that appropriate punishment is meted out, they're apt to take the law into their own hands. Vigilante justice is very rough justice because people often don't know for sure if they have the right guy or not.

HB: *But, to play devil's advocate, I could say, "What's the justification for retribution? The person who committed this act was biologically conditioned or predisposed to do this. So it doesn't make any sense to be talking about retribution."*

PC: In a certain sense you're right. That's why I said the retributive aspect of punishment is really very narrow. It's really to let the victim see that justice is being served, or else they will take justice into their own hands. But fundamentally the criminal justice system is about social safety and social well-being. We are putting people away because we fully expect that they're liable to do it again.

When you look at the law that way, it's not saying that there is no causality. It's just saying, *"Mr. Madoff, you weren't conditioned to run a Ponzi scheme; you just did it. You were no more conditioned to do that than I'm conditioned to say exactly what it is that I'm saying now. It's a choice, so you're going to be held responsible for your choice."*

I think that, in actual fact, responsibility will not diminish very much, and in the context of schools and socialization more generally, what we mostly care about is tuning up the reward system so that you end up as an adult who does the appropriate and the right thing. Very often those things involve judgment calls and that's why sometimes morality is hard.

HB: Does neuroscience have anything to say about morality? Not just neuroscience in particular, but also neuroscience vis-à-vis evolutionary biology. You give all sorts of examples in your book of how different societies view moral decisions in different ways because of their evolutionary history and because of what predisposes, or doesn't predispose, their particular society to survive. Is there a way that we could somehow ground our morality in science, as some people are trying to do?

PC: Yes and no. I think that morality—that is, the disposition to be social—is grounded in the circuitry for parent-offspring caring and bonding. From a genetic point of view, it's a remarkable thing that I will undertake all kinds of grief and difficulty, and I will make all kinds of sacrifices for my offspring. But the way to think about it is that there is circuitry in the mother for her own safety, warmth, food, and well-being, and that circuitry just changes a little bit so that it's as though the other is a part of her. That seems to be unique to mammals, probably birds, and maybe some reptiles, like alligators; and there may have been some dinosaurs that showed that behaviour as well.

But we really see it in mammals. And we also see a change in genes that produces a change in circuitry in the subcortical structures, such that if the offspring makes a squealing sound, the mother feels pain. If the baby rat falls out of the nest and squeals, the mother feels pain. She is instantly motivated to do something. I think that's the basic platform, and then with other small genetic changes the caring can expand. We know now that rats will care for others. We know that mice will take care of one another's babies too.

HB: And there are these fairness experiments that have been conducted with chimpanzees, and so forth.

PC: Yes. I think Frans de Waal was way ahead of all of us on this. His book, *Good Natured*, written in the 1990s, is, I think, one of the great moral texts of all time, and it really had a huge impact on how I thought about these things.

We are deeply social by nature. We can see this in very young children who don't like the fuzzy toy that behaves badly to the dog, but do like the fuzzy toy that's nice to the dog. These are very young children. I think it's all there, and then the motivation gets more complex and the specific conventions and social practices of a group get picked up and learned by the child.

I think we do see across cultures a very basic similarity of caring for one another and caring for offspring, despite the fact that we often have interesting differences at a relatively superficial level regarding how we handle issues of justice, or marriage, or what have you.

Questions for Discussion:

1. Is the development of an evolutionary explanation of moral behaviour the same thing as "understanding moral decisions"?

2. To what extent are "moral acts" different in kind than "socially appropriate acts"?

VII. Free Will

An age-old quandary resurfaces

HB: I'd like to dive more deeply into the question of free will now. You mentioned a little while ago that, for example, Bernie Madoff had a choice in his actions; and I would argue that virtually all of us in our everyday lives believe that. We're faced with innumerable choices every hour.

But there's an argument that I've heard addressed by people like John Searle about this issue that I've found particularly fascinating, but I didn't see it addressed head on in your book, so I'm going to ask you about it now. The argument goes something like this: suppose I believe that my thoughts, feelings, and desires, are manifestations of my brain at any given moment, which I, as it happens, do believe. In other words, I don't believe there is anything external to my brain biochemistry going on. There's no soul, there's none of that. My brain is my mind. My brain causes my mind.

I believe, moreover, that however complicated and however difficult that process is, my mind, being physical stuff, responds to the laws of physics. We can scale that up in whatever way is appropriate, whether it's the laws of chemistry, or what have you. I can imagine all sorts of emergent structures. But at any rate at the end of the day you have this physical stuff that is subject to some physical laws.

So I have my brain in one particular state, however complicated that may be, that I can map out here at some particular time, call it t_A. It's made of material stuff and I know the laws that govern these material things, which means that at another time, t_B, if you will, my brain state is going to evolve according to these laws. That doesn't seem to give me any option or opportunity to actually make a choice.

It seems to me that, according to that framework, the sense of free will that I have is actually illusory. Do you see what I'm getting at?

I *think* that I'm making a choice because when I go into a bar and somebody asks me what I would like, I think to myself, Do I want a beer or a glass of wine? There are these two options. But if it's possible to map all the stuff that I said before, then right before I'm asked that question my brain is in one state, and then there is a different brain state a few seconds later so that when I say, *"I would like a glass of wine,"* and the laws that go from that first state to the second state are deterministic. If you believe that the brain state causes the mind, that there are laws that determine that **and** that those laws are deterministic (which might not actually be the case, in fact)—it seems to me that if you accept those three things, then I *don't* actually have free will.

PC: It's a funny thing. The idea of free will as uncaused choice really comes in with Descartes. Before that, if you think about how Aristotle or others regarded choice, it was always to talk about the voluntary by way of contrast to the involuntary. So if you are involuntarily intoxicated, for example, and you do something dreadful, then that wasn't a choice. Or if you are insane—for present purposes let's just use the legal definition of insanity—then you might not be held responsible.

But with Descartes we get the idea that, first of all, there is this nonphysical soul, and part of the reason that Descartes wants a nonphysical soul is because he wants there to be choices that come about through sheer creation, with no physical involvement. That link to free choice is kind of crazy. Why would you think that free choice has to consist of creation from an uncaused condition? The idea that it's got to be uncaused to be free is a very a different way of looking at it.

Nowadays, what do people mean when they talk about free choice? By and large they mean pretty much what Aristotle did: they talk about free choice in contrast with not being voluntarily chosen. For example, if I shove you and you fall backwards, that wasn't a choice; whereas, if you sit there and you freely say to me, *"You know,*

I think your last book is really a lot of codswallop," that we think of as a paradigm of free choice, in as much as you don't have Tourette's, you're not insane, and so on and so forth. And that's as good as it gets.

The voluntariness that a normal brain provides is the voluntariness of a well-functioning pathway between prefrontal structures of the cortex and subcortical structures. That's simply as good as it gets.

Let me give you an analogy. Someone might think that there's a real difference between up and down, and that down is absolutely that way, towards the ground right underneath his or her feet. We would explain, *"No, it's actually towards the local centre of gravity."* They might say, *"Then there is no real 'down-ness'."* And we would respond, *"No, it's towards the centre of gravity and that's why you think 'down' is directly underneath your feet. That's as good as it gets."* If you want the pure, absolute 'down-ness', it simply isn't going to happen because our universe doesn't work that way. If you want absolutely, pure Euclidean straight lines in our universe, that isn't going to happen either.

In a way, the voluntariness is pretty much as Aristotle—and hence how the current criminal law—describes it. Voluntary is the default condition and if you want to convince me your behaviour wasn't voluntary, there are some things you need to show: that you have Tourette's, or that you really are insane, as defined by the law, and so forth. That's as good as it gets and if that's not good enough then all I can say is, *"I'm very sorry but, you know, we're living in the real world and we kind of have to get on with it."* I'm not going to say to my local cannibal or Ponzi schemer, *"You don't have real free will because you're a causal machine."* I'm going to say, *"You violated the law and you're going to have to stand trial, and you'll probably go to jail. End of story."* That's as good as it gets.

Questions for Discussion:

1. Are philosophical discussions of free will meaningful?

2. How might an increased understanding of neuroscience be used to influence our sense of legal responsibility?

VIII. Eliminative Materialism
What it means and doesn't mean

HB: I'd like to ask you now about "eliminative materialism", the concept that you and Paul developed. Perhaps you could start by defining it and giving me a sense of what it is, and then I'll ask you a few follow-up questions.

PC: Sure. Paul and I wanted to make a prediction. Our prediction was that, as neuroscience progresses, there are likely to be changes in the everyday psychology that we all use. His view was that the propositional attitudes would change. Let me explain what I mean by that.

If, for example, I believe that you are wearing glasses, that was understood by philosophers like Jerry Fodor and others in the following way: there is a state of my brain, a belief, that stands in relation to a bit of language. That bit of language is *"You are wearing glasses."* The idea is that that's what a belief is; it's intrinsically, essentially, and necessarily linguistic. The same can be said for desires, hopes, and so forth. Everything is mediated through language.

Paul thought that couldn't possibly be right, because we knew, for example, from the work of Lynn Nadel and John O'Keefe, that rats have this very complicated, rich, and usable map in their hippocampus that allows the rat to navigate its physical world.

HB: And, so far as we know, they're not using language.

PC: That's right. And Paul thought that their social world was probably navigated in the same way: they had a map—maybe not a three-dimensional map and maybe not in the hippocampus—but they had a map that allowed them to recognize that others had a goal, or an emotion, and so forth.

He proposed that maybe the propositional attitudes, for non-verbal humans as well as for non-verbal animals, aren't actually accurate. And, moreover, for those of us who do have language, maybe a lot of our non-conscious processing, or even some of our conscious processing (as with vision) is not propositional, it's not language-like. That was the nub of the thesis.

Philosophers went berserk. Their view was that we had said all folk psychology is wrong, and that we didn't believe that consciousness exists, which was just crazy. There was actually a guy at Rutgers who wrote the entry on 'Consciousness' for the Cambridge Encyclopedia of Philosophy and he began with the sentence, "The Churchlands, of course, don't believe that consciousness exists."

So I phoned him and I asked, *"How could you say this?"* He said, *"Well, you're an eliminativist."* And I said, *"But we actually have a theory about what consciousness **involves**. So why would we have a theory if we didn't believe it was a phenomenon?"*

HB: Talk about touching a nerve!

PC: Exactly. I don't know why the reaction was so strong. I think it struck people as very surprising, and I think the other thing was that we were just these nobodies from Manitoba who were writing this stuff.

HB: OK, I'm not a philosopher, so maybe I'm ideally placed to try to parse the expression "eliminative materialism". My understanding is that it refers to a doctrine whose adherents are desirous of eliminating currently superfluous concepts, or concepts they suspect will later be demonstrated to be superfluous, by invoking a materialist perspective.

PC: That's exactly right.

HB: If you don't know anything about this, the words sound like they mean that you're eliminating materialism, which of course is not what you're saying. It means being eliminative with the axiomatic framework of materialism and effectively saying that some of these terms that psychologists are using today, twenty years from now might be regarded as not being very well-formed, or not very appropriate descriptions of things, because a deeper understanding based upon materialism will render them inappropriate.

PC: Yes, the idea is that neurobiology would replace some of these expressions. Now, expressions like 'goal', for example, will probably not be eliminated, but others probably will.

At the time we did not appreciate that we should have thought through using that description. The description "eliminative materialism" was already in the public domain because Richard Rorty had used it, for something rather similar actually. Rorty was a very famous philosopher at Princeton and there we were, these little nobodies in Manitoba, and I think we felt that we had to connect with the conversation in an appropriate way.

Now, looking back on it, I think we would not have used that expression, because it caused such a firestorm. I think we would now say "revisionary materialism", but maybe that would have been just the same.

HB: Well, you can't make an omelette without breaking a few eggs. Maybe causing a firestorm is a good thing. It seems to me, again, as a complete outsider, that many of the ideas that these two "nobodies from Manitoba" had, are now very well-received and welcomed within, not just the neurophysiological and cognitive science community proper, but the broader philosophical community as well.

PC: Well, within some parts of the philosophical community.

HB: Perhaps it was a good strategy after all, then.

PC: Well, it's hard to know, because I think we could have come up with a better name if we had really thought about it. Although, I have to say, in the 40 years since I don't think we've come up with anything better.

HB: Well, that's a good indication that it wasn't a bad choice.

PC: Maybe. Maybe not.

Questions for Discussion:

1. Does the existence of a "mental map" in a rat's hippocampus rule out a "language-like" underlying structure? Can a map, somehow, be "language-like"?

2. Can you give some concrete examples of some present-day concepts that, with the benefit of future scientific understanding, we will come to view as unscientific and obscurantist?

IX. Consciousness
Towards progress?

HB: Let's talk a little bit about consciousness, because it's clearly not your position that consciousness does not exist.

PC: Clearly not.

HB: But what **is** your position on consciousness? What do you think it is? You talk a little bit about it in *Touching a Nerve*. Developing a full understanding of consciousness is clearly the Holy Grail, or at least *a* Holy Grail, of understanding things from a cognitive science perspective. Give me a sense of what you believe is the best explanation of consciousness that we have right now, and give me some speculations as to what you think we might be able to find out in the future.

PC: I'll try. First of all, I think one of the things we have learned from neuroscience is that there is no single place in the brain that you can point to and say, *"This is the centre for consciousness."* It clearly involves distributed networks, and not just cortical networks.

The crucial part of this story is probably located in the brain stem, which has been known for a long time to play an important role in consciousness. The thalamus in particular, especially the sort of donut-like structure in the middle of the thalamus—

HB: Let's back up a little bit because not everybody knows these terms. After all, unlike you, not everybody reading this has held a brain in his or her hands. By "cortical links" you presumably mean connections from one area of the cortex, this shell on top of the brain, to the other; is that right?

PC: Yes, that's right. The cortex is kind of like the rind on an orange, and there are vast connections from one area to the other. In fact, we now think that the cortex has a small-world organization. What that means is that it's like six degrees of separation. By virtue of this small-world organization, there are hubs, and neurons can connect to their nearby hub which can then connect to other distant hubs very quickly. And that's one of the ways that we manage to handle things like shifts in attention and processing very quickly.

That's the cortex, but the older structures are all below the cortex. In a way, they are the critical structures for motivation, feelings, emotions, self-control; and the reward system depends on these lower structures.

Below that are the, in a sense, really ancient, but absolutely fundamental, structures in the brain stem, which goes from the back of your head down into your spinal cord. In those structures there are regions that are important for keeping you alert and functioning—so much so, that if you have a stroke and those structures are damaged, you'll be in an irrecoverable coma. Those structures are also important for turning things down so you can go to sleep at night and turning them back up so you wake up in the morning.

Now, in terms of consciousness, the way it's starting to look is that the structures in the brain stem, the subcortical areas, and the cortex, all have to be coordinated in a very particular way in order for you to be aware.

You can think about it this way—or at least this is how I now think of it, but that could change in five years: there is a kind of network that provides a background that basically says, *"You're conscious. Be aware, because stuff is going on."* The particular things that you're **aware of,** like the sound of a dog barking, the smell of food burning, a pain in your knee, or a visual scene, are all switches that probably happen at the cortical level. So there's the background awareness and then there's the particular contents of what you are aware of.

HB: I've had the opportunity to talk to some other specialists in this field, and it seems to me that these ideas would mesh quite well with some of the other things that we've learned. For example, I spoke with Martin Monti at UCLA, who studies people in vegetative states and minimally conscious states, and my understanding is that, for many of these people, there are activities that are happening exactly as you're saying. I guess the explanation for what's happening with them would be that they're not conscious, but there are activities happening at a certain level, but that link isn't being made. Is that a fair description?

PC: It's sort of like that. There may be differences between individual patients. Nick Schiff at Cornell also studies vegetative states. Here's an example of someone who is in a vegetative state but might be woken up: their cortex is normal, so if you scan them there are no big holes or shrinkage. Their cortex looks normal. But their subcortical structure, in a region called the thalamus, appears as though it's in permanent sleep. And if you manage to wake it up, for example, by electrically stimulating it or, in one case—

HB: By giving the patient sleep medication, right?

PC: Right. It was Ambien actually, oddly enough. The man woke up. It was as though the thalamus had been locked into a state of very deep sleep. For years this patient just sat in a chair and then one day, after they had given him a drug that apparently had some effect on this inner part of the thalamus, it was like it reset the sleep/wake clock and he woke up. But his cortex was normal.

Now, in Terri Schiavo's case, which was a very different case of vegetative state, when you looked at her brain scan you could see that her cortex was not normal. There had been tremendous damage, huge areas of shrinkage, and so forth. That was a very different kind of situation.

But your background question was, *Does this story that I'm telling about the linkage between brain stem, thalamus, and cortex, fit with the neurological data on coma and vegetative state?* The answer is that it seems to. It also seems to fit very well with what we know about deep sleep, dreaming, and waking.

HB: So sleep is a mechanism that is somehow related to linking these systems?

PC: Within this region of the thalamus—it's kind of like a little donut inside the thalamus (the thalamus is almost like a little brain within a brain)—there are neurons that project all over the cortex. When you're awake they have a very specific firing pattern; this was discovered by a great Canadian neuroscientist, Mircea Steriade, at Laval. That very specific pattern changes during sleep. So what we think happens is that everything, so to speak, shuts down and you go into a very different state so that you're not processing information from the extremities.

It now appears that that gives the brain a chance to house clean. The brain doesn't have a lymphatic system like the rest of your body does, so it has to house clean. It appears that, in all brains, from fruit flies, to slugs, to us, there is a period where everything just sort of goes into a slow state and there's an opportunity to house clean, to get rid of all of these used up proteins and prepare for the next day. Sleep is a deeply biological thing.

HB: The second part of my question was about speculation. This is our understanding right now. But will we eventually have a coherent, reasonably complete understanding of consciousness? Will that happen at some point? And, if so, when do you think it might occur?

PC: I think we'll get the basic story, but I don't know when. There are many fundamental, open questions in neuroscience, so it's very hard to predict. As John Searle often puts it, *"It's a biological phenomenon."* So predicting that you'll never know seems to me to be a very rash prediction. I would expect that we'll understand a lot of it. But bear in mind that the word 'understand' means that we may just understand part of it; it comes in degrees.

It's interesting that we don't really understand yet, in a complete way, how genes work, but consider the progress we've made. I think we'll eventually understand a huge amount about what's really involved in consciousness. Every five years you see new techniques and ways of addressing very fundamental questions about the brain.

Questions for Discussion:

1. Do you believe that scientists will have a clear understanding of the mechanisms of consciousness in the next 30 years?

2. Why do you think that so many consciousness researchers are focused on patients in a coma or vegetative state? What are the strengths and weaknesses of such investigations?

X. Summing Up
Some key questions

HB: If I were an omniscient being—which sadly I'm not—and I could answer any one or two questions of yours, with respect to this area, what would you ask?

PC: One of the things that's still very much out of our ken has to do with the basic principles on which brains function. If you think about the motor system, it's critical because that's where evolution has a chance to act, because it's all about your behaviour. Evolution can't directly act on your perceptual systems. It can only act on the degree to which your perceptual systems inform your behaviour so that you can behave in such a way as to survive (or not survive).

Now, it looks like the motor system is not going to be understood in terms of representations. We think of vision as representational. We think of my brain as right now representing your blue shirt or your spectacles, so that there is a kind of mapping between inside and outside. But we don't think of the motor system as acting in that way. We think of the motor system as a kind of dynamic system. So one of the deep puzzles is, if we think of vision as representational, how, in terms of the evolution of nervous systems, is it going to fit with this nonrepresentational system? How does that work?

Maybe we're thinking about vision in the wrong way. Perhaps when we chat with each other we can say that I'm representing your blue shirt, but if we think of it from a neurobiological perspective, maybe it's not all about representations. I don't know. That's one of the fundamental things.

The other fundamental thing we really don't understand about the brain is that, if understanding something, perceiving something, or making a decision, depends on networks distributed across the brain, how is that coordinated? You don't have networks for every single little thing that you perceive. How do you get so much out of just your brain?

HB: And how do those networks form to begin with, and why those networks and not other one?

PC: Yes. So that's something we don't understand: how is this all working without a coordinator? And the coordination problem is not just about connections across the cortex, but across the cortex, the subcortex, and the rest of your brain. That's a deep principle. And that's why it's often helpful to look at simple animals—fruit flies, slugs, mice—who really aren't all that simple, but if we can figure out some of the basic principles from these animals, almost certainly evolution has conserved those principles and then elaborated on them in the case of humans, so we can get closer in that way.

If we get closer, in the case of humans, then we have a shot at understanding things like schizophrenia, autism, and so forth. That's huge. When you think that, over their lifetime, roughly one percent of the population will have had a brush, or more than a brush, with schizophrenia, that's huge. I do believe we'll get there, but it's not easy.

HB: Very good Anything I haven't asked? Anything else you'd like to comment on?

PC: I don't think so.

HB: Well, thank you very much. This has been a most enjoyable conversation, Pat.

PC: Thank you. You were very well-informed and asked great questions.

Questions for Discussion:

1. What does Pat mean, exactly, when she distinguishes between "representational" and "dynamic" systems?

2. Might studying simpler biological organisms, such as fruit flies or slugs, sometimes lead us astray in understanding or appreciating key human biological principles?

3. Are there any dangers associated with the development of a deeper understanding of how the brain works?

Continuing the Conversation

Readers are encouraged to get a deeper understanding of Pat's thinking through her popular books: *Conscience: The Origins of Moral Intuition*, *Braintrust: What Neuroscience Tells Us About Morality* and *Touching a Nerve – The Self as Brain*, which goes into considerable additional detail about many of the issues discussed here.

Free Will

An Investigation

A conversation with Alfred Mele

Introduction
Down to Earth

The notion of "free will" has a long and turbulent history over the past few millennia, directly impinging on such flashpoint issues as divine oversight and individual moral responsibility. It played a lively philosophical role during the Reformation and Counter-Reformation, as some believed that the predestination inherent in most strands of Protestantism skirted precipitously close to a denial of free will—more than enough, indeed, for its attackers to keenly leap to that conclusion and its defenders forced to vigorously mount the intellectual barricades to deny it.

But by the time Isaac Newton had resoundingly demonstrated universal laws to conclusively link terrestrial and celestial mechanics over a century and a half later, the philosophical ground had shifted considerably: suddenly, there were those who speculated if God himself might be constrained by such a comprehensively deterministic system. After all, people wondered, once the "clockwork universe" had been set in motion, what real wiggle room did even He have?

These days, of course, the ground has shifted yet again, with "free will"—long consigned to the domain of university philosophy departments as a dusty, irresolvable piece of metaphysics roughly equivalent to speculating on how many angels can fit on the head of a pin—suddenly emerging as an issue of keen interest, if not active debate, among a general public fascinated by rapid advances in neuroscience. Which certainly stands to reason: as brain imaging technology improves, it becomes less and less of a stretch that we might, somehow, begin to meaningfully "measure" our actual thought processes and finally get a firm handle on whether or not our intuitive convictions of free will are actually fact or fiction.

Into this re-energized landscape steps Alfred Mele, the William H. and Lucyle T. Werkmeister Professor of Philosophy at Florida State University and a highly engaged member of the "free will renaissance", authoring a spectrum of books such as *Autonomous Agents*; *Free Will and Luck*; *A Dialogue on Free Will and Science*; *Free: Why Science Hasn't Disproved Free Will*; *Aspects of Agency: Decisions, Abilities, Explanations, and Free Will* and *Manipulated Agents: A Window to Moral Responsibility*.

For Alfred, logically enough, the first thing that must be done to successfully wade into these exciting new waters is to take the time to identify what we're actually talking about. And so, in his own charmingly accessible way, he outlines three currently in vogue positions on what it means to have free will at all, invoking a "gasoline model" by referring to them as "regular", "mid-grade" and "premium".

> *"For those who choose "regular", a sufficient condition for having free will is that you're sane, rational, well-informed and autonomous. You make a decision on the basis of the information, a rational decision, and nobody's coercing you or compelling you. There's no gun to your head. That is enough for the decision to be free, according to this regular view of free will.*

> *"But then, you see, this is where we get to what I call "deep openness". Somebody might think, Yeah, but that's not enough, because it could be that really that was the only decision you could have made, given the laws of nature and the initial conditions of the universe.*

> *"And there are those who want to add that into their definition—I call that the ambitious or "mid-grade" level of free will—that this needs to be taken explicitly into account. In other words, if it can be deduced that the laws of nature have determined your behaviour than you don't have free will. According to the "regular" definition, the laws of nature aren't considered. All that matters there is if you are rational and not coerced and then you have free will.*

> "Now the third one, the spiritual one, adds something even more to all this: that there's a soul at work somehow.
>
> "I should say that these aren't just abstract characterizations—there are many people who genuinely believe this. I've done some research on it and others have too—controlled research—and it looks like maybe 25% of the people in the Southeastern US think that free will requires souls. But that's only 25% of people and it's just the Southeast US.
>
> "So most people are in the other two groups."

The fact that Alfred eschews "just abstract characterizations" turns out to be a highly revealing aspect of his approach. Not content to merely sit in his office and ruminate, he is strongly motivated to develop his arguments by regular appeals to empirical understanding, leading him to consistently weave data from neuroscience, social psychology and public opinion polls into his reasoning process.

Given all of that, it is hardly surprising that for Alfred, a key concern is how current and future insights might be directly applied to improve our world.

> "One thing I'd like to know is, How much would educating people about the existence of these effects influence their future behaviour?
>
> "I give a lot of talks to undergrads these days, and I'll often speak about situationism. And at the end, I ask them what they think they'll do the next time they're in a crowded mall and they see a young kid crying and looking lost or watch an old person fall. And I tell them that, on average, what the effect predicts is that they'll just walk away like everyone else. But the key questions are, What will you do? and What should you do?
>
> "And I think that, itself, can make a difference. But this is just my intuition. If we did a study like this, or several studies like this, then we'd have good evidence about it."

Intuition is good. But evidence is better. Even for philosophers.

The Conversation

I. Becoming A Philosopher

From Aristotle to Irrationality

HB: So, philosophy for you: was it something that you were interested in for a long time? Would you describe yourself as a particularly "philosophical" child, say? I'm not so much asking you if your philosophical career was somehow predetermined—we're going to get there soon enough, I suspect—but more generally assessing your early interests and tracing your trajectory into the field.

AM: As a youngster I didn't even know what philosophy is. But, yes, I think I always had philosophical interests. I was raised in a religious household—Catholic—and I would just wonder how all these different things could work. I didn't go to Catholic school until eighth grade, but I went to catechism when I was young and I learned that you're supposed to love God more than your parents.

I asked my brother, Ron, one day: "*Do you love God more than Mom and Dad? It doesn't make any sense to me, because I don't know God and I know Mom and Dad. How am I going to love Him more?*"

And I remember Ron, who's a year younger than me, telling me "*Yes, I do, because that's what I'm supposed to do.*" But I just found that I couldn't do it, so that was one of the things I worried about.

HB: Did Ron come into the equation too? Did you start measuring your love for Ron with respect to your love for your parents?

AM: No, I wasn't clever enough back then. I remember trying to figure out how gravity worked using a globe and toy cars. Why do these cars just stay on the globe? Why don't they fly off? So, there were things like that. Maybe most kids don't think about them, I don't know.

I got interested in philosophy in college. I started off as a math major. I liked math a lot; I still do. Then I took a math course that had a logic component, which I really enjoyed, so I took a logic course which was offered by the Philosophy Department and thought that was really cool.

And once I was in the Philosophy Department I looked around to see what other courses there were and the one that really got me hooked was one on Plato and Aristotle. These guys had views about everything, integrated views, and I thought, *My goodness, this is amazing!*

At the same time I was also taking some psychology courses, but this was at a time when behaviourism was dominant in much of psychology—certainly where I was—and I just didn't find it all that exciting.

I was very interested in human behaviour right from the beginning in college, but I wasn't able to get what I wanted from psychology. But I could, in a way, from Plato and Aristotle.

So after I took this Plato and Aristotle course, I decided to be a philosophy major. Then I went to graduate school in philosophy and wrote my dissertation on Aristotle and Aristotle's theory of human motivation. Back then I could read ancient Greek pretty well.

HB: How did you pick that up? You must have had to do quite a bit of extra work there.

AM: In graduate school. I went to a Catholic high school, so I learned Latin then; and then in college I learned Spanish. But neither of them would qualify for the language requirement in graduate school at the University of Michigan.

HB: Spanish wouldn't qualify?

AM: No. I think because I was in philosophy. If I'd been in a different discipline, maybe it would have been okay, some different discipline.

HB: You needed what? French?

AM: Yes: French or German. So I took French. Then I started studying classical Greek, which is the hardest of those.

HB: So I've been led to understand.

AM: Originally, for perhaps my first three or four years out of graduate school, I thought I would just be an Aristotle scholar. Of course, there are people who do that: they just write on Aristotle and interpret his ideas. But I was always really interested in some of these issues he was talking about, and I started having views of my own about these things.

After a while I thought, *Well, now it's time to branch out and tackle those issues directly*.

HB: Such as?

AM: Well, my first book is called *Irrationality*, and it's on what's called weakness of will, self-deception and self-control. Aristotle had a view on weakness of will, so did Plato, and they both had views on self-control. Self-deception they didn't have much to say about: Aristotle had nothing that I can think of, while Plato only had one sentence.

HB: What was the sentence?

AM: "*The lie in the soul is the worst thing of all.*" That's about it. "The lie in the soul" is lying to yourself.

HB: Right. He doesn't really explain how it can happen, though. It's just bad.

AM: That's right. And I wanted to know how it could happen. Weakness of will is a matter of being convinced that it's best to do one thing, but then not doing it and doing something else instead when you could have done the thing that you believed to be best.

For example, you believe it's best not to have a third bottle of beer because you're about to drive home, but you have one. Or, you believe it's best not to eat a second dessert, but you eat one anyway.

Plato actually thought, "*This can't happen unless the guy doesn't really know what's best.*"

HB: You can't knowingly desire something which is not in your best interest, right? Isn't that a Platonic idea?

AM: That's right. Which means that if you do go ahead and do that then you must either have been compelled to do it or you didn't really know. Aristotle had a more relaxed attitude, but generally speaking he seemed to think that there had to be some defect in your knowledge in order to do this.

And I just thought, *Well, this sort of thing happens all the time. It happens to me. People tell me it happens to them. How does it actually work?*

And to figure that out, I didn't want to do it just purely hypothetically or purely intellectually. I wanted to look at data. So I did: I looked at lots of data. From quite early on in my career I was really interested in how we could apply scientific findings to these age-old philosophical questions.

HB: Where did these data come from for this particular project?

AM: I got a lot of use out of Walter Mischel's data on self-control in children. He wanted to know under what conditions four-year-old kids could delay the longest and wait for their preferred reward over a less-preferred one.

Under one set of conditions, you get kids to say whether they like marshmallows better than pretzels, or pretzels better than marshmallows. Then you leave them both out, and you tell the kids who prefer marshmallows, "*You can have the pretzels whenever you want, but in order to get the marshmallows you have to wait for the experimenter to return. So you can signal for the experimenter to come back and get the pretzels, or you can wait.*"

When both rewards are present, the kids waited an average of less than a minute before they called the experimenter back. But when both of the rewards are covered up so they can't see them, they delay much longer. So is it just that they can't see them? Is that what's doing the work?

Then they performed an experiment where they showed them slides of the pretzels and slides of the marshmallows, and it turns out that they delay even longer in that condition than when both are covered up.

So what was going on?

Their theory was that these objects have a kind of "informational value" and a sort of "exciting, pulling value". When you're looking at the real objects themselves, you're directly subjected to the excitement, the pull. But when you're just looking at the images, it's different: you're just getting the information of what's on offer that enables you to say to yourself something like, *These things are better than those, so I'll wait.*

At any rate I got a lot of data from that, from Mischel's work.

For self-deception, I started by thinking about parallels with two-person deception. Suppose I'm determined to deceive you into believing something. That means that I know the truth and I want to get you to believe the opposite.

Now let's put all of that in only one head so that I am deceiving myself: I know the truth and I'm somehow going to get myself to believe the opposite. How's that going to happen? After all, presumably I know what I'm up to.

Before I continue, maybe I should say a little bit about how I got interested in self-deception to begin with.

That first book of mine that I'm talking about, *Irrationality*, was published in 1987—I wrote it in '85-'86; it takes a while for these things to come out—but in 1981, when I was just working on Aristotle and nothing else, I was invited to be a commentator on a paper on self-deception by a major philosopher.

I agreed to do it, but I didn't know anything about self-deception. I didn't even know that it was a philosophical topic. So, I started to read a bunch of journal articles on self-deception, including some by this guy, to try to figure out what was going on.

And after having read the articles I came to the conclusion that, the stuff that we call self-deception probably doesn't actually involve intentionally deceiving yourself.

When we say, "*Oh, that guy's self-deceived*," what sorts of things do we have in mind? It's situations like this: Everyone in the community knows that some 14-year-old kid is using drugs, but the parents just sort of block out any evidence which might point them in that direction.

HB: It's a form of denial.

AM: Yes, I think denial is involved in a lot of it. Here's another example. People who know this couple have good evidence that the wife, let's say, is having an affair; and they believe that she is.

The husband has a lot of that same evidence, but he just turns his attention to other things and he never comes to believe that she's having an affair, at least not until it's way too late, say.

That's what people mean when they talk about self-deception, which doesn't involve this really paradoxical feature of knowing the truth and getting yourself to believe the opposite.

So the first thing is to explode that paradox. And the next thing is to look into the mechanics of how it all actually works. And in order to do that, there's a lot of stuff that's relevant.

There's evidence of something called "confirmation bias": that if you're testing a hypothesis you naturally tend towards looking for confirming evidence rather than disconfirming evidence. So, that's one thing that kicks in. Beliefs are driven a lot by the salience of the things you're thinking about.

When the parents are thinking about their kid whom others say is on drugs, what might become salient for them would be happy memories of him playing in the sand with his toy trucks. So they think, *Well, a kid like this couldn't act like that.*

And on and on. There's more data, too.

HB: OK, but is this still a philosophical issue at this point? I mean, from my perspective, the act of making the argument that self-deception is not, in fact, equivalent to some paradoxical process that is strictly analogous to two-perception deception combined in the head of one person seems like a philosophical sort of undertaking.

But once you've done that—once you've declared this is what we mean by "self-deception" and here's how it differs in kind from what one might naively conclude it to be—then aren't you taking it out of the realm of philosophy and turning it over, as it were, to the psychologists and neuroscientists and so forth?

AM: Well, I think of "philosophy" very broadly: there just aren't many limits. So, after having exploded the paradox in the way I suggest, I recognize that people are still going to wonder, "*Okay, so how does this happen, exactly?*"

Then I can draw on this empirical work and explain how it happens, which actually makes the exploding of the paradox better, because now I've put an alternative phenomenon in its place and I explain how it happens. So hopefully people will now think: "*Hey, that's great. I'm going for this. I'm going to give up this old model of self-deception and I'll move on to this new one.*"

There's statistical data that's interesting in this connection, too. There was a survey done quite a while ago of students who were taking the SATs, and they would rank themselves on certain traits and skills. There were about a million of them.

25% ranked themselves in the top 1% of the ability to get along with others, and you see this happening over and over again—people systematically overestimating themselves trait after trait, ability after ability. So what is going on there? Why do so many of us do this?

HB: Speak for yourself.

AM: Well, actually, it turns out that the most realistic people about themselves are depressed people. What we don't know is, *Are they depressed because they're realistic, or does it go the other way around?*

HB: They might turn out to be the only well-adjusted people in the world.

AM: Now, a little self-exaggeration, or whatever, is probably a good thing, I think. But you can see how this just pushing things a little bit further and we get into something that you might even call self-deception. In fact, you might even want to call that itself self-deception.

HB: Well, I certainly would. When 25% of the people seriously believe that they're in the top 1% of something, there's definitely a misalignment with reality, so self-deception is the word I would definitely choose for 24% of them.

Questions for Discussion:

1. To what extent might self-deception be linked directly to our neurophysiological state? For an intriguing perspective on how non-autistic students taking Adderall leads to significantly skewed perceptions of accomplishment, see Chapter 8 of **Exploring ADHD** *with UC Berkeley psychologist Stephen Hinshaw.*

2. To what extent might self-deception be a reflection of larger cultural factors? For an examination of how American students consistently overestimate their abilities, see Chapter 10 of **Mindsets: Growing Your Brain** *with Stanford University psychologist Carol Dweck.*

3. Do you agree or disagree with Howard's concern that self-deception, as described by Alfred Mele, belongs primarily in the domain of cognitive science rather than philosophy?

II. Outlining The Problem

Defining "free will"

AM: That first book, *Irrationality*, on weakness of will, self-deception and self-control led to my second book, *Springs of Action*, which was a book about the springs of human behaviour: what causes us to do what we do? It's interesting and complicated, but I have a causal theory about how all that works.

So then I thought, *Okay, I do have a general understanding of how human behaviour is produced, but it's human behaviour in general—intentional behaviour*. And I thought, *Well, now it's probably, at last, time to tackle free behaviour*.

I'll have to use just a little technical terminology now. There's this old dispute between philosophers who say that free will is compatible with determinism—determinism has to be defined in a certain way for this to make sense, it's a standard way in philosophy—and philosophers who disagree.

When I was a student I'd read about free will. I even taught a bit about it in undergraduate courses. But I always thought, *This is kind of stale*, so I wanted to wait to work on it until I had a thought, a new thought, something that would be exciting.

Springs of Action was published in 1992, and just a little bit later it was time for me to apply for my second round of sabbatical grants. I had one to write the first book, *Irrationality*, and so this would have been about six years later.

It was funded; and it was a book on free will. I called it *Autonomous Agents*, because free will suggests—to some people, anyway—something spooky or mysterious or spiritual; and I just wanted to keep all that under wraps, especially the will part.

So, I just used "autonomy" as a name for free will, and went from there. What I did, because I didn't want to settle, or try to settle, this dispute between the compatibilists and the incompatibilists-

HB: You didn't want to try to go there?

AM: No. And I never have.

HB: Well, that I can understand.

AM: Yes, I like to try to do things I think I have a reasonable chance of succeeding at doing.

HB: Fair enough.

AM: That's just part of my style. So what I did was to develop two different theories, two different full-blown theories of autonomy: one for people who are happy to say that it's compatible with determinism, and one for the others. They overlap in lots of ways. There's a difference that's crucial to that distinction.

I had an account of self-control, too, a whole theory of self-control. So I spelled that out in Part One of the book, and then asked, *What can we add to self-control to get autonomy?* And the second half of the book was about that.

The reason self-control isn't enough for autonomy or free will is that, while you can be very self-controlled in the sense that you resist all desires that are contrary to your better judgements, and you're really good at that, you stick to the plan, hypothetically—this is, after all philosophy—it could be that the system of values that drives all your self-controlled behaviour is brainwashed in.

And if it's brainwashed in, then it looks like you're not an autonomous agent. It looks like somebody else, ultimately, is in charge. So, that was the idea of that book, which was my first one on free will. Well, half the book was on free will, although I called it "autonomy".

HB: But behind this is this whole idea—I think it's from Schopenhauer, right?—that you can do what you want, but you can't really change what it is that you actually want to do.

AM: Yes, that is one of the ideas here. Mine is different, though. I think you *can* actually revise your values by reflecting on them. So, you could care a lot about something, and then eventually you ask yourself, *Is this thing worth caring about as much as I do?* And you could come to see that it isn't; and then you won't care about it as much.

HB: Well, one of the things that has frustrated me—long frustrated me, in fact—about these sorts of discussions is that all too often people are talking about different things when they're throwing the same words around, the same nomenclature.

In particular, when people say "free will", it's not clear what, exactly, they're talking about, just as when they say "determinism". And while it's reasonable to expect that different people will agree on different things as a general rule, it's particularly problematic, and particularly likely to have all manner of divergences of opinions and theoretical constructs when you can't really get a clear sense of what the terms actually mean to begin with.

In your book, *Free*, you spend a lot of time at the very beginning highlighting those very points. You explicitly say things like, "*Okay, different people mean different things. This is what I mean, and here's an interpretation based upon this analysis of what these words mean.*"

At the very beginning of the book, you talk about three different types of notions of free will, making an analogy between three different types of gasoline.

There is the premium-grade free will that has some notion of weird spirituality aspect of it, a mid-grade free will that you designate as "ambitious" and a regular free will that you call "modest".

Perhaps you can elaborate on these distinctions.

AM: Let's start with the first, basic version of free will—if we use the gas station analogy, it's regular. So, a sufficient condition for having free will is that you're sane, rational, well-informed and autonomous.

You make a decision on the basis of the information, a rational decision, and nobody's coercing you or compelling you. There's no gun to your head. That is enough for the decision to be free, according to this regular view of free will.

But then, you see, this is where we get to what I call "deep openness". Somebody might think, *Yeah, but that's not enough, because it could be that really that was the only decision you could have made, given the laws of nature and the initial conditions of the universe.*

And there are those who want to add that into their definition—I call that the ambitious or "mid-grade" level of free will—that this needs to be taken explicitly into account. In other words, if it can be deduced that the laws of nature have determined your behaviour than you don't have free will. According to the "regular" definition, the laws of nature aren't considered. All that matters there is if you are rational and not coerced and then you have free will.

Now the third one, the spiritual one, adds something even more to all this: that there's a soul at work somehow.

I should say that these aren't just abstract characterizations—there are many people who genuinely believe this. I've done some research on it and others have too—controlled research—and it looks like maybe 25% of the people in the Southeastern US think that free will requires souls. But that's only 25% of people and it's just the Southeast US.

So most people are in the other two groups.

HB: Right.

AM: I'm no expert on souls, so I don't have much to say about that. I focus on the first two kinds.

HB: OK.

AM: Perhaps I should define determinism now.

HB: Go right ahead.

AM: Okay, so this is the way we think of it in the free will literature. If a universe is such that a complete description of the universe at any point in time together with a complete list of the laws of nature entails all other truths about the universe, then the universe is deterministic. That's what it is for it to be deterministic.

So for the "regular" free will people, you can have free will in a universe like that because for them it doesn't matter whether you could have done otherwise or not given the same past and the same laws of nature. All that is required to have free will from their perspective is that you're sane, rational, well-informed, and uncoerced—that's enough for free will for them. So in this case free will *is* compatible with determinism.

HB: OK.

AM: Now, the mid-grade guys say, *"No, that can't be right. In order to have free will, it needs to be like this: that given exactly the same past and exactly the same laws of nature, you sometimes make a different decision than the one you actually did."*

And one way I suggest to try to picture it is by having access to some sort of "rewind button" on our lives. So the world plays out until now, and I suddenly decide to raise my right hand. Now the mid-grade guys would say, *"That decision you just made to raise your hand isn't free, no matter how sane and rational and uncoerced you were, unless you could have done something else, given everything exactly as it was."*

So now we imagine being able to rewind time, say 10 milliseconds and then waiting to see what happens—doing that a bunch of times. And then for me to have free will from their perspective, then in at least one of those reruns some other possible course of action will occur—like raising my left hand.

HB: OK. So that one makes perfect sense to me. I suppose I'm going to have a problem going forward—and I should come clean about this right from the beginning—because to me, this is the only game in town.

Let me put it another way. I don't live in the Southeastern US, and for all sorts of other reasons besides I'm not particularly interested in trying to sort through what these so-called "premium-grade" guys are thinking, so like you I'm quite prepared to move on from that.

But unlike you, I'm not really super-motivated to look at things from the perspective of the "regular" guys either, because it seems to me that they are simply avoiding the actual issue.

In short, this strikes me as being completely equivalent to my longstanding problem with the so-called "standard compatibilist" position: I'm convinced that they are simply not addressing the issue and just defining it away and sticking their heads in the sand.

So perhaps you can help me see the light here.

AM: Okay.

HB: Let's start with two premises. One is materialism: that everything around us is made of material stuff and is thus subjected to the laws of nature. The other is that those laws of nature are deterministic. Now, of course, you don't have to believe any of those. Clearly your "premium-grade" guys don't believe in strict materialism, and there are also those—although you haven't addressed this yet—who might well be of the view that the fundamental laws of nature are not, in fact, deterministic.

But my guess is that both the "mid-grade" and "regular" types accept both of those premises—or perhaps we should simply make a further categorization into those "mid-grade" and "regular" types who do, because for the moment anyway, those are the only one's I want to be talking about.

AM: Okay.

HB: OK, so here's my problem. I no longer care what you call yourself—"mid-grade", "regular", whatever—all that matters to me is that I'm addressing people who have agreed that they buy into my two initial assumptions: that we live in a materialistic universe and the laws governing those material objects are deterministic in precisely the way you described a moment ago.

And that implies that if you take the example of someone coming to a fork in the road, say, it simply cannot be the case that if you were to push the rewind button a zillion times, you would ever get a different result.

So conceptually, in my view, there is no issue whatsoever: you simply ***don't*** have free will. Period. Now you may well not like that. You might find it deeply uncomfortable and recognize that the logical implications of that understanding lead to all sorts of different approaches to societal legal codes and associated moral responsibility that you simply don't want to consider, being convinced that the likely result of doing so would be full-throated anarchy (which would, of course, be predetermined anyway, but whatever). You might find it all sufficiently uncomfortable that you would find yourself saying things like, "*Of course I have free will!*" by explicitly redefining what you mean by "free will" according to some completely different criteria, like to what extent someone is holding a gun to your head or whether you like elephants or what have you. You might call yourself a "compatibilist" or a "grand piano" or something else entirely. I don't care: all you're doing is avoiding looking things straight in the eye. The only way out, I'm convinced, is to reject one of those two initial assumptions.

AM: Okay, that makes good sense what you said. Now, there are some different replies to this. Some you won't like, one you might not have thought about. I'll start with one that you probably won't like: some compatibilists, really are claiming that determinism, just as we've described it, is compatible with free will.

HB: Well, I think that's completely incoherent. So convince me otherwise.

AM: Okay, they're not disagreeing with you about what determinism means.

HB: Okay.

AM: So some will say, "*No, the only sense in which you need to be able to have decided otherwise, in order to have free will is that if conditions had been slightly different, like if you'd had different reasons to do things, then you would have acted differently.*"

HB: But that just means that the initial conditions would have been different.

AM: That's right.

HB: But everyone knows that different initial conditions might lead to different results. Nobody disputes that. The whole issue is to what extent the *exact same* initial conditions will lead to different results. Which I maintain that, under a fully deterministic framework, is impossible. And not just impossible, exactly, but actually *tautologically* impossible—literally an oxymoron. But "impossible" is probably good enough.

AM: Well, what these guys are saying is, "*Look, all that matters is how a guy thinks about things: Whether he's sane, whether he's rational, whether anybody's pushing him around.*"

And then they say, "*If it's important to you to think about being able to do otherwise, well, the sense you're thinking about it doesn't matter, what really matters is just whether the guy is receptive to reasons, so that if reasons had been different, his behaviour would have been different.*"

Now, a lot of people don't like this at all. I can tell you don't.

HB: No, I don't. I think it's utter nonsense and a complete avoidance of the question. But let me be even more blunt—you didn't think I could be, did you?—and say that this doesn't make me happy in the slightest. In fact, the reason this whole issue exercises me isn't because I'm determined to prove that we don't have free will—I'm quite convinced that we *do*, in fact. But you're not going to make me happy just be redefining up as down and down as up.

AM: Okay, let's move on to the second point. So you made a choice—your fork in the road you mentioned a moment ago. And we want to know: *Did you do it freely?*

HB: Exactly. That's what I understand by free will.

AM: And what you might say is that you didn't do it freely unless you could have chosen otherwise.

HB: Right.

AM: Okay. Now I'm going to invoke an old thought experiment. It's from Harry Frankfurt, 1969. But we'll do my version of it because his has a certain glitch in it that you'd probably spot, so we're going to do mine.

HB: Okay.

AM: Okay. So now I imagine some potentially mind-controlling guy on the scene who implants in my head a certain process that sort of ticks away like an alarm clock and is set to cause in me, at a certain time, a decision to steal your car.

HB: All right.

AM: But it just so happens that I'm thinking about stealing your car anyway. This universe now is going to be indeterministic.

HB: Well, if you assume an indeterministic universe...

AM: That's okay though. You want to see the point.

HB: All right.

AM: So I'm thinking about whether to steal your car or not. It turns out that at just the moment that the process that was implanted in my head would have caused my decision if I hadn't decided on my own, I decide on my own to steal the car.

Now, I decided on my own. The universe is indeterministic and nobody's pushing me around. I'm saying I'm rational. So it looks like what we should think is, *Hey, that's a free decision. He freely decided to steal the car,* but I couldn't have done otherwise in the thought experiment than decide to steal the car, because if I hadn't decided on my own to do that this process would have caused me to decide to do that.

Now this little thought experiment—well, it's part of a bigger paper—led lots of people to think that you don't really need to be able to do otherwise in order to have acted freely. There's a case in which you can't.

There was John Locke's old example of a locked room. This one isn't fully persuasive—it is up to a point until you start thinking a little bit further—but there's a guy in a room and he's having a nice conversation and he thinks about leaving.

He decides to stay and he stays, but it turns out he couldn't have left because the room was locked and he had no way out. So he stayed freely, even though he couldn't have done otherwise than stay.

Now, if you don't like this, the move is going to be, *Okay, he stayed. But what is important here is that he decided to stay, not that he could have acted successfully on a different decision—to leave.* So what Frankfurt does in the thought experiment is to sort of move the locked room into the head.

HB: Well, perhaps we're going too far down the rabbit hole here, but I think that the problem with all of these sorts of thought experiments is that there's a lack of basic understanding of what we mean by "the laws of physics" and "initial conditions" and "end states" in a deterministic universe. They include the room, yourself, the whole spiel.

My sense of what is happening here is that people start positing what they think is "extra stuff" like locks on doors or gremlins with mind-controlling apparatus or whatever, but that doesn't actually do anything because once you posit those, they become part of the big picture. They're not "extra" at all. By definition.

AM: Compatibilists realize all that. And what they say is, "*We don't believe that that's incompatible with free will.*"

HB: OK, let me try again. As I've said, I've heard this word compatibilist thrown around many times, and it's never made the slightest bit of sense to me. Understand that I'm not saying, "*This is a position that I recognize is coherent and defensible but I simply don't happen to agree with it*"—there are lots of those around too—but something much stronger: "*I simply have no idea what these guys are talking about.*"

So here's my view. There are these laws of physics that affect everything—you, me, doors, keys, gremlins—and I can characterize any overall state of my universe—or at least my small corner of it—uniquely somehow. Physicists would talk about something like "a point in configuration space", say. And these laws of physics are deterministic: they take me from any one initial state to any one final state with no ambiguity—that is, one point in configuration space to another.

So now look at my fork in the road. I've got going to the right—call it A—and going to the left—call it B. They represent two different points in this configuration space.

And what I mean by free will is that from the same initial condition right before the fork in the road—call it Q in my configuration space—I can somehow opt to influence things so that I end up at either A or B.

AM: Holding the past and the laws of nature fixed.

HB: That's right. In fact, the laws of nature can change, they just can't change in a nondeterministic way. But that's probably an unnecessary complication. And the past I'm definitely not touching.

AM: OK.

HB: So again, I don't see any way out here if you buy into these assumptions. Of course, it's horrendously complicated because, properly speaking, what I mean by "initial conditions" and "end states" and "points in configuration state" has to, as I mentioned earlier, include *me* too (and lots of other things and people as well). Which is to say that it has to, properly speaking, include my "brain state", which I'm assuming can somehow be rigorously quantifiable in principle. Now there might be all sorts of reasons to suspect that such a thing is not, in fact, possible (I actually believe that, as it happens), but my understanding is that's not what these people are arguing. They're somehow willing to accept all of that—that there is an all-encompassing deterministic law of nature which inevitably maps every initial state to a unique final state—and somehow they just wave their hands around and shout "compatibilist" and convince themselves that the problem has gone away.

AM: All right. Then I think the short answer is you're making an assumption that the compatibilists reject and the assumption you're making is that in order to do a thing freely, you have to have been able to do otherwise, holding the past and the laws fixed.

HB: Exactly.

AM: They reject it.

HB: How do they reject it, exactly?

AM: Well, here's one way. The way a lot of philosophers think about free will is that it's a necessary condition for moral responsibility. So now they have these things tied together.

HB: Sure.

AM: Now you might think about practices of holding people morally responsible in the actual world.
    And then you might think, "*Well, heck, maybe the actual world **is** deterministic. Would these practices still make sense?*" And you might

well convince yourself that they do, that it makes sense to convict guilty people provided that they're sane, and so on.

HB: Well, as a practical method, absolutely. I'm certainly not arguing that we should stand up and declare, *"Guess what? We've just discovered that there's no free will after all so it makes no sense to punish people for things they couldn't avoid doing. Get rid of all the lawyers and open up all the prisons!"*

Well, not the prison part, anyway.

But that's not a philosophical metaphysical argument. That's a practical argument.

AM: It's a practical kind of argument that might get people—and has got quite a few people—to think, *"Well, really that's all there is to free will: a measure that would underwrite deserved praise and blame."*

HB: Oh, for God's sake. How is that any different from justifying my belief in the Great Pumpkin because it makes me feel better?

AM: Now remember my own view. Early on, I said, *"I do not take a position on this dispute between compatibilists and incompatibilists."*

HB: Well, I recognize that I've been quite combative. It's not, as you know, personal. It's just that sometimes I have a hard time remaining neutral on issues, particularly when they simply make no sense to me—which, as I said, is a very far cry from not happening to believe in them.

Of course I'm sensitive to the link between free will and morality. That's really, in a way, the whole **point**. It's not that I can't recognize that our entire framework of morality would collapse if we were to deny free will, it's in fact precisely *because* I recognize that link that this issue is such a particularly vexing one. But you don't meaningfully solve a problem just by defining it away because it makes you feel better which seems a pretty weaselly and inappropriate thing to be doing. That's like redefining a manned mission to Mars by defining my living room as "Mars". OK, we went to Mars. Where next?

So just to be super-clear, I am certainly not suggesting that we do anything different now in terms of changing our assumptions about human morality and responsibility for individual decisions, which I not only think would be hugely impractical, but also—as it happens—wrong. Because, as I've said before, I'm intuitively convinced that we **do** have free will. But I recognize that demonstrating that necessarily involves wading into metaphysics and not simply saying things like, "*It would be bad for our society if this wasn't the case.*"

AM: Well, from their perspective they're just saying, "*Look, you make this certain assumption about free will. Why do you make it? We think that if you think about things in a more down-to-earth way where you tie free will to moral responsibility, you find it really difficult to believe that nobody would be morally responsible for anything just because determinism is true, then you start pulling the bar for free will lower.*"

So that's how they think about it. Now I know people who just won't go for it no matter what.

HB: Well, maybe now would be a good time to admit that despite how animated I'm getting during this conversation, it's not actually the case that I am lying awake in a cold sweat every night worrying about free will.

But there *is* a problem, insofar as I feel that I have to recognize the strength of the challenge—which is significant—in order to jibe my intuitive conviction with a very strong argument in the other direction.

So for me the approach to take is, *Okay, how do you address that? How do you find a way out? How do you respond to the actual argument from the other side?* Personally, my strategy would be to focus on determinism.

There's also, of course, the perfectly reasonable approach, in my view, to say, "*This is a really hard problem that I can't solve at present but I'm going to focus my attention on other things.*" There are, after all, lots of really hard problems out there, and life is short. And if I'm honest, that's pretty well the approach I take with this one. So I'm not saying, "*Anyone who doesn't roll up their sleeves and dedicate the* rest of their lives to definitively cracking the problem of free will once and for all is a weeny!"

I'm just saying, "*Don't pretend to have solved something when you haven't done anything of the sort.*"

AM: Well, we'll get up to the second level of free will pretty soon, which will bring in indeterminism, but maybe I can add one more comment here.

So Eddy Nahmias, who's a terrific guy—he used to be a colleague of mine here at Florida State—has done empirical studies on whether ordinary people are compatibilists or incompatibilists.

And you don't want to ask them, "*Hey, is determinism compatible with free will?*" Most people mean by determinism, "that thing that is **incompatible** with free will"—they don't have clear thoughts about it.

So what he does is to write up little stories, one paragraph stories, in which it's clear that determinism is true of the universe without using the word "determinism". And then he describes a person doing something and asks, "*Did the person do it of her own free will? Did she have free will at the time? Does she deserve to be blamed?*" Questions like that.

One story he uses is a supercomputer story where the supercomputer can predict, solely on the basis of its knowledge of the laws of nature and the initial conditions, everything that everybody will ever do. It's done this thousands of times. It's always been right—that kind of thing. So that universe is deterministic.

And then he'll have people do moderately good things, moderately bad things, or neutral things in his stories before asking people questions like, "*Did he do it of his own free will?*"

And it turns out a majority of people will say, "*Yes.*" So their answers are consistent with what compatibilists say.

HB: This is supposed to convince me?

AM: Well, no. But I'm saying this to you because you might start thinking, *Well, why **do** I think this? Is it just some idea I picked up in school long ago? Am I out of touch with the people and with some specialists?*

And then, once you start thinking about that, you might become a bit more flexible. I know I'm really flexible about this because I can see these two different ways of thinking about things: a compatibilist way and an incompatibilist way.

And where did I come by my ideas about what free will means? Well, maybe I had some in Catholic school, I don't know in high school, but I sort of get them by reading the opposing sides.

Questions for Discussion:

1. Are you convinced or unconvinced by Howard's objections in this chapter? Do you think he is too critical? Intolerant? Reasonable?

2. Which of the three types of "free will gasoline" that Alfred describes do you find yourself most naturally associated with?

*3. To what extent is it relevant what the majority of people in a society think about a philosophical issue such as free will? A related perspective can be found in Chapter 5 of **Meaningfulness** with UNC philosopher Susan Wolf when she describes Aristotle's famous "endoxic method".*

III. Neuroscience

Benjamin Libet stirs things up

HB: I'd like to return to some specific issues in your book, *Free*, because we've sidestepped a lot of them, quite possibly because I was indulging myself by ranting far too much.

There are various people who look at the question of free will from the perspective of conscious versus unconscious actions rather than through a more metaphysical or moral and legal prism that we discussed earlier.

In particular, I'd like to talk in more detail about these very influential experiments by Benjamin Libet that went a long way towards convincing people that free will doesn't exist, based upon their definition of free will corresponding to a conscious, as opposed to unconscious act.

Meanwhile, social psychologists often invoke issues of free will in a similar conscious versus unconscious context when they discuss to what extent people are influenced by the values and pressures of those around them, from peer pressure to cultural values to subliminal advertising.

AM: Right.

HB: Perhaps it makes sense to start with the Libet experiment.

AM: Yes, let's talk about that.

So, the task was to flex your wrist whenever you want as you're watching a really fast clock—the spot on it makes a complete revolution in about two and a half seconds.

Meanwhile, you're hooked up for EEG—which means that readings of electrical conductivity on the scalp are being taken—and your wrist is also hooked up to an electromyograph, so that when your muscle starts moving that can be detected and measured.

You need to flex at least 40 times to get data that are usable. So you're sitting in the chair, you're watching the clock, and what you're supposed to do after you flex is report on where the spot was on the clock when you first became aware of your urge or intention to flex you wrist.

HB: Because subjects are simply being told, "*Flex your wrist whenever you want, but just pay attention to when you decide to do that,*" right?

AM: That's right, that's the basic idea. And when subjects are regularly reminded to be spontaneous—that is, not to plan in advance or think about when to flex—you get a ramp up which can be summarized by the following graph, with the EEG readings on the vertical axis and the time going forward on the horizontal axis, with the time they actually recorded their wrist flexing on the clock at the far right.

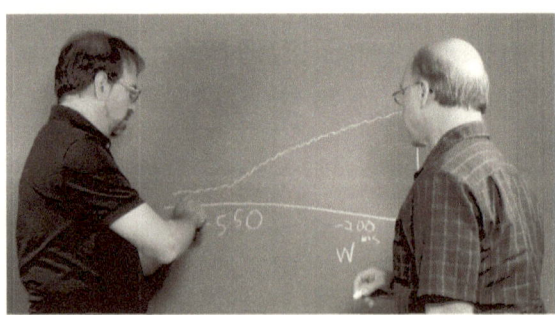

So the time at which the muscle in the wrist starts moving is typically around −550ms—a little more than half a second before it actually flexes—and then you start getting a ramp up in the EEG readings, with the average time of first reported awareness of this urge or intention at about 200 milliseconds before the muscle starts moving, which is called "W time".

So what Libet says is when the EEG ramp-up starts, **that's** when the decision is made, and he takes these reports that are made after the flex seriously and says, *"But people don't become aware of those decisions until this later time W, so the decision was actually made about a third of a second before the person became conscious of it."*

So then you get the connection to free will, with the claim being, *"Well, look, unconscious decisions can't be free. They have to be conscious decisions in order to be free."* And since Libet believes that he has shown that these decisions are made unconsciously, we don't have free will.

But is he entitled to assert that the decision is made half a second before, at that −550ms point, as opposed to something happening there that's part of a causal process that perhaps results in a decision later on?

Well, first off, we can distinguish between decisions you make now to do things now—like "flex now", which is what's happening in these studies—we call those "proximal decisions", and decisions you make now to do things later, say, deciding now that you're going to have dinner at 7:00 pm.

So he's talking about proximal decisions; and what we'd want to know is how long it takes them to cause muscle motion. That's one thing we'd want to know—we'd want to get independent evidence about that.

Now, if you think of a decision to do a thing as just a little action of forming an intention to do it, then if you can get information about how long it takes proximal intentions to do things with your hand, say—to cause muscle motion—that would be very useful.

Well, there are reaction-time experiments where you know that when you get the go signal, what you're supposed to do is flex your wrist, for example. So you can measure the time between the emission of the go signal and the muscle burst in those examples.

Now, what you'd want to do is find an experiment—or perform your own—where people are watching a clock, because that's going to divide attention and slow down reaction time.

Back when I was first turning my attention to these issues, when I was writing my book, *Effective Intentions*, I didn't have any big grant money to do such an experiment, so I looked for a study like that which had been done.

And I found one—it was by Patrick Haggard and Elena Magno, as I recall. Subjects were watching a Libet clock, and they were doing a "go signal reaction time test". And the average time between the emission of the go signal and the beginning of muscle motion was 231 milliseconds. And it takes, of course, a little time to detect the go signal.

So the time between intention acquisition and muscle burst is going to be less than that. And that could be how it is in Libet's case too: that the intention doesn't really come up until around the W point somewhere, and back at around −550 ms there's a pre-intention causal process up and running that may or may not issue in an intention around W.

Now, this is a point I've made and persuaded a lot of people of, and there's more to say about it: you get similar readings when I'm watching you about to do something and we're taking readings from me and I know that you're about to do it. We get curves that look a bit like this if we average over many trials.

Then some people will say, "*Well, maybe you're right about that. Maybe that's not a decision back there at that −550ms point. Maybe the decision doesn't happen until around W, but back at −550ms we've hit the point of no return for the making of that decision. Once that's happened, there's no way the process is going to be stopped.*"

Well, is that really the point of no return? Well, what you'd want to know when you're thinking about that is, *Do we ever get curves in Libet experiments where the curves start out looking the same but there's no subsequent muscle burst at the end of it?*

Well, it turns out that Libet's data don't let you look at that, because when you do studies like this you need something to signal the computer to make a record of the preceding second or so of brain activity—to store it so they can do the back averaging, do the statistics. And what he used to trigger the computer to do that was the muscle burst.

HB: So by definition in his process there will always be a muscle burst there.

AM: That's right: because that's the trigger. So we don't have any good reason to believe that the point of no return has been hit at that point (around −550ms) either.

And regarding points of no return: well, there are "stop signal" reaction time studies too, just like there are "go signal" ones. The appropriate task would be something like, *Flex when the spot hits the 9:00 o'clock point on the clock, unless the clock colour changes from blue to red, say*.

And you can move that stop signal closer and further from the designated time and people will stop. Stop signal reaction time on average is about 200 milliseconds too.

Now, if you can do that with an external signal, what about an internal signal? Something like, *"Yeah, I'm tempted to flex then, but don't do it,"* which brings us to the topic of Libet's veto.

Essentially, he believed that once you become aware of your decision you have about a hundred milliseconds to veto it.

I could go into more detail about his arguments there, but maybe I should stop there for now—that's essentially his position.

HB: Well, the details are in your books, *Free: Why Science Hasn't Disproved Free Will* and *A Dialogue on Free Will and Science*. The last thing I'd want is to eat into your book sales.

I'd like to move on to discuss the impact of his results. My understanding is that when they were first released they caused—and in some circumstances are still causing—a real firestorm of hyperbole when it comes to people talking about whether or not we actually have free will, what's been proven and not proven. Simply the fact that Libet's results have been so broadly used by so many people for so many different positions needs to be emphasized, I think.

AM: Yes.

HB: And you do a very good and important service, I think, in your calm and dispassionate interpretation of things.

In particular, you say things like, "*Look, even if it can be shown that for some types of decisions there are factors that are going on that we're not consciously aware of—and it's not clear from all of this that that's even true—but even if it is, we have to ask ourselves: 'What does that actually show?' Well, it means that for some types of decisions, we are not consciously aware of all stages of why it is that we act in a particular way.*"

You explicitly point out that these experiments are only looking at a very, very small—and, for the most part, hugely irrelevant—percentage of decisions that we're making as conscious beings, like when to "spontaneously" flex our wrist or pushing this or that button in a highly artificial circumstance. They have nothing to do with the normal sorts of decisions that any reasonable person would assume would have something to do with free will, like whether I should go to this university, as opposed to that university, or thinking rigorously through some complex process—you give the example of all the things one has to do just to buy a particular seat on a plane.

These are the things that most of us mean when we talk about "making decisions", so the implication that every decision we make would necessarily have something to do with these results by Libet, or all necessarily governed by unconscious acts of the brain, is hugely unwarranted.

AM: Yes, it's an amazing generalization. It's part of Libet's view. The generalization claims are there in the paper and his book. He says, "*Yup, that's the way it's working here. Decisions are made unconsciously in our experiment, and we can generalize this to all decisions.*"

As I said, he thinks that once you become aware of your decision you have about a hundred milliseconds to veto it, but you can never consciously initiate an action, you can only consciously stop it.

And this generalization is unwarranted, as you say. Now, another point to keep in mind is that the subjects are instructed here *not* to think about when to do this task.

HB: Right, which is exactly what you don't want to do for free will presumably; we're talking about making a conscious decision.

AM: Right. When they're careful not to do it, you get results—it's called a "readiness potential" like the one we were just describing. When they do think about it, you get a different one, one with a longer tail.

So another question to ask is, *How much are decisions that you don't think about at all, but just make—like spontaneously deciding to flex your wrist—like these important decisions that we're talking about?*

Well, not very much; which makes it even harder to generalize from findings about one to findings about the other. And as you say, I even actually dispute the claim about the findings for Libet's case about where the decisions are actually made.

Now, there are later experiments done with different technology, but they all suffer from the problems that we're talking about, including the generalization problem.

So why did it create such a storm and so much interest? Well, it did and it didn't. The first Libet paper on this was published in 1982, and then there was a *Behavioral and Brain Sciences* paper published in 1985—that's a big and important journal and articles are published with lots of commentaries. And there were lots of commentaries.

And then the scientific interest, it seems to me, sort of petered out for a while. Philosophers still talked about it sometimes—I was writing papers on it quite a while ago. But then Patrick Haggard, a very good neuroscientist in London, resurrected the Libet-style research and did some more. And that really brought it back to prominence.

So what's the worry about free will, exactly?

It's pretty obvious to me that the generalization claim isn't legitimate. There are my worries about even correctly interpreting the

Libet results. And there are worries about the timing too. This turns out to be a really hard task—I was a subject in one of these experiments, as it happens. So there are all those worries.

Well, one thing that seems to be going on among some scientists is that they think of free will as requiring something immaterial, something nonphysical as a cause of behaviour.

I know, it's puzzling. They're thinking, *Well, look, we're getting hard evidence that it's brain events that are causing decisions*.

HB: How does this lead to an immaterialist worldview?

AM: Well, Libet had an immaterialist view. What he wanted to do was to find evidence of a power of consciousness that swoops in from outside and generates decisions.

HB: That was his agenda, as it were.

AM: Yes, that's what he *really* wanted to do. And he thought he found some evidence for it in the veto. Let me just read you a quotation from a neuroscientist, Read Montague, from a 2008 article in *Current Biology*. He's telling us what free will means.

"*Free will is the idea that we make choices and have thoughts independent of anything remotely resembling a physical process. Free will is the close cousin to the idea of the soul. The concept that you, your thoughts and feelings derive from an entity that is separate and distinct from the physical mechanisms that make up your body. From this perspective, your choices are not caused by physical events, but instead emerge wholly formed from somewhere indescribable and outside the purview of physical descriptions. This implies that free will cannot have evolved by natural selection as that would place it directly in the stream of causal connected events.*"

HB: Well, tautologically, if you take it outside of the domain of physics, then it's not going to be subjected to the laws of physics. I'm guessing that he's one of those 25% in the Southeastern United States.

AM: And he's not the only one. I have other quotations from other scientists who are claiming that free will requires that souls are at work.

HB: You seem to have a particularly generous definition of the word "scientist". But that's just my opinion.

AM: Well, from this you can see why people would think that a study that suggests strongly that the brain is heavily involved in decision production would lead them to claim that there's no free will. But there I think, it's all gone off the deep end. We shouldn't think of free will like that.

HB: Yes. I mean, once you give up on materialism, all bets are off. I mean, you can do anything—you can have angels hovering around making particles do strange things at CERN.

For the record, I'm not making some ironclad metaphysical claim that I can prove or disprove the existence of any spiritual beings or angels or anything like that.

All I'm saying is that it seems pretty clear to me that scientists shouldn't be concerned with any of that. The business of science should be all about investigating sufficient causes within the laws of nature as we best understand them. Once they're moving away from that, it seems to me that they ain't doing science anymore. If that's their agenda, then they should get another day job.

AM: I see. That's pretty good. Before we leave this topic, I'd like to make a couple more points about this whole experiment.

Again, what you're doing here is reporting, using the clock, on where you figured the spot was when you first became aware of your intention. Now, imagine that we're systematically off with that, because usually we're not trying to time when we made our decisions, we're just making them.

So imagine that we're 50 milliseconds off. We're always late. Well, is that going to stand in the way of free will? What if a lot of conscious processing went into the production of the decision? Isn't that good enough? I think that just doesn't matter for free will, the lateness of it.

Also, the task really *is* very artificial. I try this with audiences sometimes when I give talks on this. I say, *"Okay, now for the next 90 seconds or two minutes, just flex your arm like this every once in a while, as you're listening to me, and I'm going to ask you a question about it later. But try to keep track of what I'm saying."*

So they'll do it—and it looks weird to me because I'm looking at all of them doing this to me as I'm talking to them. And then I'll ask them, *"How many of you were aware when you flexed that you had an intention to do it just then?"*

And almost nobody says yes, because these sorts of things we can do automatically—we don't need to make conscious decisions to do them. We just have a plan to do them every once in a while and we carry it out.

So what you're doing when you do this experiment is forcing people to be conscious of something that they wouldn't normally be conscious of.

Now, in my case, it wasn't really an intention or an urge. I mentioned that I was a subject. I gave a lecture to the motor control unit at the National Institutes of Health on free will and neuroscience.

The plan was that first I do the lecture, then I'm a subject in the experiment, then they take me out to dinner. After the lecture, I went to the lab, sat in the chair and got wired up. I knew what I was supposed to do: flex whenever I wanted to and then report after I flexed where the spot was on the clock.

What happens is that the clock runs for another revolution or sometimes a revolution and a half or two after you flex, then it stops and you get a cursor, and you move the hand to the point on the clock where you thought it was when you first became aware of your intention or urge.

But no urges came to mind, no intentions, nothing was happening really, except I was thinking, *How do people do this?* and *What am I going to do?* Because I don't want to look like a jerk, and I do want to have dinner.

So the plan that I hit on was that I would say, "*Now,*" silently to myself every once in a while, and I would treat that as a "go signal"—or you could say as an expression of a decision—and I'd flex in response to it and I'd try to remember where the spot was on the clock when I said "*Now*" silently to myself.

I thought it was going pretty well and then Mark Hallett, who was in charge of the lab and the guy who invited me to give the talk too said, "*Al, you're flexing in too wimpy a way. We're not getting good readings. You need to flex in a more aggressive way.*"

So here I am, just saying "Now" to myself silently every once in a while, trying to flex in an aggressive way, trying to keep track of the clock.

And those flexes I could have made without being conscious of any intentions at all, if I didn't have the instruction to report. So the instruction generates something in your consciousness that there wouldn't be without those instructions. That makes it even harder to generalize from findings about cases like this to actual, thoughtful decisions.

HB: Again, I think your inclination to bring down decision-making processes and question our tendency—or at least some people's tendencies—to make broad, sweeping, generalizations from them is very important.

I mean, the idea of firmly ascribing "consciousness" or "lack of consciousness" to all decisions is something that I think jars with pretty well everyone's personal experiences.

We've all, I suspect, been in the situation of driving somewhere, or taking the bus somewhere or whatever, and then thinking to ourselves afterwards, *I don't actually remember all the steps involved in doing this. Did I really change the gears? Did I really deliberately choose which route to take?*

It's clear to everyone, just from our anecdotal experiences, I think, that the light between "conscious decisions" and "unconsciousness decisions" can be pretty fuzzy and complicated depending on the decision.

But that hardly implies any deep metaphysical statement about how we're all fundamentally automata or being "directed by our brains" or anything like that.

These are clearly interesting results that demand more attention and more reflection to fully interpret, but I think the idea of straightforwardly generalizing to some of these sorts of conclusions, especially when you add in things like immaterialism—I mean that's just plain whacky. I don't understand why more people aren't drawing attention to that.

AM: Well, that is something I've thought about. If you put it in a "news" context—which I think is related to your question—weird news generates a lot more attention than normal news.

So if someone says, *"Oh, you have free will, don't worry about it."*—who's going to write about that? Most people already assume that they have it.

But this weird news that, *"Maybe you don't!"* generates excitement; and that excitement might help to generate grant money that helps to generate more work of this kind.

Of course, I believe that there are interesting payoffs to the actual neuroscientific work, whatever the conclusions drawn may be, and these experiments are definitely worth doing.

HB: Unquestionably.

AM: But for many people, much of the motivation can be traced back to a conviction that the soul is responsible for free will and brains aren't. But once it gets that far, it's not interesting anymore. You just lose interest in it.

Questions for Discussion:

1. To what extent have advances in neuroscience impacted our sense of free will and moral responsibility? For an additional perspective on this issue, see Chapter 2 of **Neurolaw** with Duke University legal scholar and philosopher Nita Farahany.

2. How might the prevailing view of many neuroscientists that the brain is constantly engaged in predicting events be essential to correctly interpreting the results of the Libet experiment? Readers interested in more details of "the predicting brain" are referred to Chapter 6 of **Minds and Machines** with Miguel Nicolelis, Chapter 3-4 of **Constructing Our World: The Brain's-Eye View** with Lisa Feldman Barrett and Chapters 2-4 of **In Search of A Mechanism: From the Brain to the Mind** with Chris Frith.

3. To what extent can we be genuinely said to be acting "consciously" when we are "mind-wandering"? For a comprehensive treatment of this issue, readers are referred to **Mind-Wandering & Meta-Awareness** with UCSB psychologist Jonathan Schooler.

4. Do you agree with Howard that science shouldn't concern itself with doctrines like immaterialism? Is it possible, even in principle, to develop a scientific proof of the existence of God?

IV. Social Science

Eating away at our sense of autonomy

HB: Let's move on to the social science aspect we alluded to earlier: in particular, I'd like to look at social psychology and examine the implications of their distinct definition of "free will".

AM: Sure. There's a style of study called "situationism" that indicates that the situations in which we find ourselves have a really powerful influence on our behaviour, in ways that we don't recognize actually.

Perhaps it's best to start with a study on what's called "The Bystander Effect". It was motivated by what happened to Kitty Genovese in 1964 in New York City, where apparently she was murdered on a public street in the evening, and many people could have witnessed it from their apartment windows, but according to news reports nobody called the police. And you'd wonder, *Why not? It's an easy thing to do. The person needs help. Why not do it?* So a pair of psychologists decided that they would try to study this phenomenon.

Here's one of the experiments—it's very nicely done. You get subjects to come in, and you lead them to believe that they're going to have a conversation with other college students about college life and problems encountered in college life.

The experiment is set up in such a way that you believe that you are interacting with the student remotely whom you believe to be in a neighbouring room, and you are told that in the other room there is either nobody else who can hear the student—you are alone—or two other people, or five other people.

Now, what's actually going on is that in all cases it's just you and there's simply a tape recorder in another room. Subjects are told that the microphones work in such a way that when one person is talking over it, nobody else can talk. Nobody else can be heard.

What happens is they play a tape recording that goes on for two minutes and five seconds of somebody who says that he's having a lot of trouble. He thinks he's going to have a seizure, is really worried, starts stuttering and so on.

And the question they are looking to address is, *Does it matter how many people you think can also hear the voice? Does that influence your behaviour?*

And it turns out that when people think that they are the only ones who can hear the voice, 85% of the people leave the room and go get the experimenter before the tape is done playing. When they think that one other person can hear the voice, the helping rate goes down to 62%. And when they think four others can hear it, it goes down to 31%.

So it seems that it's the case that knowing how many people can hear the voice has, on average, a huge effect on your behaviour, despite the fact that all of us believe that it shouldn't—that the right thing to do is to rush off and get the experimenter no matter how many other people we think might have also heard it. So that's one type of study.

Then there is Philip Zimbardo's Stanford prison experiment, a classic social psychology experiment in which people volunteered to take part in a mock prison life where some of the people would be guards and some of the people would be prisoners.

HB: Arbitrarily divided.

AM: Right, arbitrarily divided into one camp or the other. And the ones who were selected to be prisoners were actually picked up in police cars at their residences and driven to the Palo Alto Police Station, and then from there to the prison, which was in the basement of the Stanford Psychology Building. The experiment was supposed to go on for two weeks, but they had to cancel it after six days because things were really getting out of hand: a lot of the guards became bullies and had prisoners do things like wash toilets with their bare hands and all other kinds of nasty stuff.

And one thing that's really interesting about it is these prisoners just stayed there and they could have left. They could have said, "*No, I'm done with this. This is a stupid experiment. I'm gone.*"

There was no way to predict which guards would become bullies. Nobody could predict it. So it seems like just role-playing has an enormous influence on behaviour.

HB: Right. So my response to this, you might be relieved to know, is quite different than some of my previous concerns.

On the one hand, I am convinced that these sorts of studies in social psychology that you mentioned—and, of course, there are many more, but those certainly seem to be some of the most famous ones—are real, compelling and very important.

Moreover, I would go so far as to say that to a large extent what they are highlighting—the influence that other people have on our behaviour—has been egregiously and mysteriously underappreciated with typically disastrous consequences.

As it happens, I had the opportunity to talk at length with Phil Zimbardo (*Critical Situations*) and he took great pains to point out the very explicit and obvious comparisons to the Stanford Prison Study and what happened over 30 years later at the infamous Abu Ghraib prison in Iraq, which he described as "the Stanford Prison Study on steroids".

I certainly agree that we need to pay attention to these issues, not only most obviously to try to understand how larger sociological phenomena might arise—like mass populist movements and genocide—and thus be prevented, but also how to best train and educate people so as to decrease all manner of terrible individual acts, from human rights abuses to high-school bullying.

So I am certainly *not* saying that these sorts of studies, or this sort of research is irrelevant or unimportant—anything but.

But on the other hand, to return to the subject of today's conversation, I'm not convinced that it actually really has much to do with free will either.

There is, after all, a huge difference between saying, "*It is a scientifically demonstrable fact that under such and such circumstances people tend to behave in this particular way, and we should establish our training systems and organizational structures explicitly with this in mind to minimize the likelihood of bad things happening,*" and saying, "*This is an issue with free will.*"

AM: OK, that's interesting. Well, here's one way to think about it: think of "control" as coming in degrees. You might start off thinking that you have full control over what you decide to do all the time, and then the more you learn about things, the more you begin to appreciate that you have less control than you thought you had—there are other things that you're not aware of that influence your decisions.

Now, I certainly don't see that control shrinking all the way down to zero. Take the Bystander Effect study that I mentioned. Even when the person thought that four other people could hear the voice, 31% of them *did* help, which makes you wonder about the other 69%—or at least, say, the extra 54% that helped in the first instance, when the person thought he was alone.

For those people, the Bystander Effect actually made it more difficult for them to help than would have been the case otherwise. But does it make it impossible? No. But it just seems harder, on average, to make good decisions under conditions like this.

HB: And, to reference a point you've emphasized several times during the course of this discussion, it's also dependent on what sorts of decisions we're talking about. There's a big difference between unthinkingly following along with our friends or our peers when they're engaged in some inappropriate behaviour or helping someone when she's in distress—or, of course, deciding when to flex our wrist—and deciding where to go to college or which job offer to take.

So once again a key problem seems to be the desire of some people to generalize some particular result for some subclass of decisions to necessarily all decisions all the time.

We didn't talk today about "subliminal advertising", but you have thought about this, too, of course—as many of us have. I don't pretend to know where the current state of science is on this issue, but I'm perfectly happy to assume for the sake of argument that it can be demonstrated that in some specific situations for some specific products subliminal advertising can be objectively deemed to be effective on some specific people. Which might lead us to all sorts of conclusions, like regulating against the presence of such techniques, or developing better awareness programs so that people can train themselves to resist, or whatever.

But it certainly doesn't make me think that every conceivable decision I make I have no control over or something like that. Which means that, for me at least, I can effectively take "free will" off the table, here—it becomes a sociological, psychological or cognitive science-type of thing.

Do you see what I'm saying? As far as the principle of free will goes, I've already pushed that aside. I've convinced myself that, *Yes, I have control over the situation*. Maybe I have to work harder to find ways to exercise that control and not be led unwittingly down the garden path by people or situations, but I certainly don't have to worry, philosophically, about any decisions somehow "being made for me".

AM: Yes, I agree entirely.

So maybe before people reflect more deeply upon it, they would think, *I have total control over everything I decide, and I'm not influenced by anything I'm unaware of.*

Well, we have good evidence that things aren't like that. So some people might be disappointed. Some people like you might say, "*Well, I thought it was like that, but it turns out that there are lots of influences on what I decide. But still in the end, most of the time, it's up to me what I decide.*"

Now there are people—not so much theorists, but often people I hear questions from when I give talks—who think that free will has to be an "all or nothing" thing: either you have it and you're using it all the time or you don't have it at all.

And if somebody has *that* way of thinking about free will, then they might think, *Well, since some of these scenarios demonstrate that there are times that you don't have full control, then that must mean that I don't have any control.*

HB: Well, that certainly follows if you accept the initial premise—that it has to be either all one way or all the other way. But that's a crazy premise. It's completely unfounded.

AM: That's right.

Questions for Discussion

1. In what ways is it meaningful or appropriate to make a distinction between free will as a "philosophical problem" and free will as a "social problem"?

2. Might a deeper understanding of situational effects lead us to become *more* responsive to others' needs in certain circumstances than we might otherwise be? Those interested in this topic are referred to Chapter 8 of **Critical Situations** with Stanford University psychologist Philip Zimbardo, where he discusses his Heroic Imagination Project that was explicitly created to do precisely that.

V. Next Steps

And mid-grade investigations

HB: Let's talk about future work for you. I understand that you've recently started a 3-year project on self-control, so I expect you'd like to talk about that, but I'd like to start things off here by asking you a different sort of question: If I could give you an infinite amount of money and five years, say, to conduct whatever experiment you'd want to perform, do you have any that would spring to mind?

AM: Yes, actually, I do.

Regarding the Bystander Effect, for example—or any of these situationist effects that we're talking about—one thing I'd like to know is, *How much would educating people about the existence of these effects influence their future behaviour?*

Imagine we would spend time educating people about the Bystander Effect and then, a couple of weeks later, say, follow it up with a similar type of experiment to what we were just talking about—maybe a fake injury or something. And we could compare the results of that study with those of a group of people who weren't subjected to that initial education about the Bystander Effect.

HB: So that be your control group?

AM: That's right. I would like to think that educating people about the Bystander Effect would make people less likely to display it. I would think those people would think, *Gee, there is that effect. I don't like being pushed around by situations like that. So I know what I should do: the next time I'll do the right thing.*

I'd like to think it goes that way, but I'd like to see evidence of it.

HB: And if it does go that way—and I suspect you're right, I suspect it would, at least there'd be some statistically significant effect—then that would certainly argue for a more systemic coherent education process writ large in our society for these very issues.

Clearly we would like to do whatever could be done to decrease the likelihood that people don't ignore others who are in peril. So if you can show that specifically targeted educational efforts can reduce that in the future, that is clearly in all of our best interests.

AM: Yes, I agree entirely. I give a lot of talks to undergrads these days, and I'll often speak about situationism. And at the end, I ask them what they think they'll do the next time they're in a crowded mall and they see a young kid crying and looking lost or watch an old person fall? And I tell them that, on average, what the effect predicts is that they'll just walk away like everyone else. But the key questions are, *What will you do?* and *What should you do?*

And I think that, itself, can make a difference. But this is just my intuition. If we did a study like this, or several studies like this, then we'd have good evidence about it.

HB: Have you witnessed any attempts to make a more comprehensive theoretical framework for these sorts of situational effects, rather than taking them one by one?

Let me try to be clearer with what I mean. I could imagine that there might be some philosophers, or social psychologists, or perhaps collaborations between the two, who say, *"I'm working on this big foundational theory of how human behaviour is influenced by situational factors and my goal is to be able to get phenomena like the Bystander Effect or Phil Zimbardo's Stanford Prison Study to somehow pop out of my larger theoretical framework as specific instances of my core principles."* Do you ever hear people saying things like that?

AM: They might be doing that, but I'm not aware of it. Now, some people have drawn the conclusion that really *all* of our behaviour's entirely driven by situations, so we never act freely. I've seen that.

HB: No. Really? Hold on. Back up. So, *all* of our behaviour, everyone, 100%, is driven by situations?

AM: Yes. So there's no free will. But the data don't support it because we have people behaving differently in the same situations.

HB: Just one study you would think would be able to just shoot that one down.

AM: Yes. So then what they'd have to claim is, "*Well, these people are such that when they're in this situation, they help and the other people aren't.*" But that's just empty.

HB: Well, I was anxiously awaiting you saying something like "that's just empty"—you had me worried there, because your tolerance seems to be so much higher than mine.

Well, we've been speaking for quite a while now, Al. I could go on, but maybe now's the chance to turn it over to you and ask if there's anything that we've missed, or you'd like to talk more about.

AM: Well, we never really did get to that second type of free will, the mid-grade. We could just do a little bit on that just so people know how it's supposed to work.

HB: I'm happy to do that.

AM: Okay. So here's the idea. So remember that first-grade, "regular free will", is compatible with determinism. It doesn't say that it requires determinism, but it's compatible with it.

HB: So you say. See, that's the one *I'd* call "empty".

AM: Right: you hate that one. Okay. So for people who hate that one, I have this other one. What we have now is an indeterministic set-up so that the relevant laws are just going to be probabilistic.

And you're sometimes going to have this indeterminism in decision-producing streams right up until the moment of decision so that, holding the past and the laws fixed, although you decided this way, you could have decided that way—without any monkey business like, *If things had been different, you would have decided differently.*

What I do then is just build that into the "regular free will". You add an ingredient to it, and the ingredient is this indeterminism: take away the determinism. So it's just this change, which maybe you'd be happy about.

And then what you wonder is, *Okay, does real decision-making work in this indeterministic way?* And we don't have conclusive evidence one way or the other, because this is a really hard thing to measure. And the indeterminism there would be actual physical indeterminism—nothing fancy.

HB: Well, but it *is* different from the way we approach most physical circumstances. When you say "nothing fancy" it's worth pointing out that much of the time—certainly not *all* the time, but most of the time, say—when we think about things evolving according to certain physical principles and physical laws, we believe it to be deterministic.

AM: Yes, at the macro level. But when people say that, I respond, "*Right, that is really just most of the time.*"

So think about how a Geiger counter works. It's detecting beta decay. Beta decay is supposed to be indeterministic. If it detects it, the counter clicks. You hear it. That's a macro event. But it's an undetermined macro event. And there could be things like that in the brain. And there are some biologists who think they've found evidence of genuine indeterminism in little fly brains.

Now, we can't get into all of those details now. But suppose they're right, and there really is indeterminism there. Then that could be part of our evolutionary heritage. It may just be that the brain works indeterministically. Maybe that's just the way it is.

Now, *why* would it? Perhaps it turns out to be useful for certain purposes. You don't want to be overly predictable to enemies, say. Now, one way to achieve not being overly predictable would just be a deterministic system that has built into it different ways to go on different occasions. But another way would be to have an indeterministic system that can respond differently to the same stimuli.

HB: OK, well, now I'm going to flex my intolerant muscles again, I fear (freely and deliberately, of course).

Once you start asking question like, *To what extent does a brain working this way as opposed to that way assist us in being able to avoid predators?* you are, it seems to me, couching the whole ball of wax in a deterministic framework.

AM: I'm not entirely sure. The background here is now we're assuming the universe is not deterministic.

HB: Okay. So maybe the issue is that there are different, subtle aspects of what is meant by determinism or indeterminism. Of course when we talk about natural selection or the survival of the fittest or different evolutionary trajectories that result in some worlds replete with dinosaurs and other worlds replete with people who like Boy Bands, there certainly seems to be a "random" or "indeterminate" element to things.

AM: Yes, we talk about chance selection. Actually, it's consistent with determinism because it could just be that the chance is epistemic in the sense that, we can't do the calculation, we have no idea.

HB: Well, that's my point. There is often a confusion between true, inherent indeterminism—the exact, same initial conditions can logically result in two different end states—with the "knowledge in principle" arguments like, *"There's no way we could ever have everything figured out in such a way as to have precise knowledge of those initial conditions in the first place—every molecule tagged, every gene specified, every incoming mutation-causing gamma ray accounted for."*

AM: Well, the universe could actually be indeterministic—in the way that a lot of people in quantum mechanics say—and evolution could work in an indeterministic way, and then decision-making could work that way too sometimes.

And that's what the "mid-grade people" want: you get to a certain point in the process and you decide to do a certain thing, but everything being the same up until then, you could have decided to do something else.

And for that you do need indeterminism: if you believe that it's brains that are making decisions, you do need indeterminism in brains. So you really need those laws, the relevant laws, to be probabilistic rather than exceptionless.

Now, that won't be enough for people who think you need even more control, those in what I call the "premium-grade" category—

HB: OK, but let's please ignore those immaterialist people. I mean, this is the 21st century, after all—surely we're passed dualism by now. If you want to officially include those guys in your books because you're a professional philosopher, more tolerant, more open, less empty, live in the American Southeast, whatever it may be—that's obviously your right.

But as someone who is determined to keep this discussion on a scientific basis here on planet Earth, I'm going to strongly push back on this one.

AM: OK, I think that's fair enough. And again, that's the one that I don't really say much about because I'm not an expert on souls.

HB: One last thing, perhaps, that I almost always seem to eventually arrive at in any discussion I have with people about free will. My favourite thinker on free will—perhaps because he is one of the very few I actually think I understand—is the philosopher John Searle.

And, perhaps unsurprisingly, my interpretation of his position is very much the one that I have been articulating—with a certain degree of belligerence, I appreciate—throughout this conversation: that being a materialist who believes in deterministic laws governing the universe is logically incompatible with free will, which leaves you two choices if you want to preserve free will: either abandon materialism—which, as you have observed, I clearly don't want to do—or abandon determinism.

So you might think that this is not a problem at all, particularly given that I am a physicist and for a long time now physicists have been forced to come to terms with the idea, through things like quantum mechanics and chaos theory, that the underlying laws of nature need not, in fact, be fundamentally deterministic.

Which is certainly true enough. But what this usually amounts to is people simply throwing out words like "Schrödinger's Cat!" or "The butterfly effect!" into these discussions as if that solves everything; and when I reflect upon it, I'm far from convinced that any of that actually solves anything at all.

Because I am neither a cat, nor a Geiger counter, nor a butterfly, nor a quark, nor a polarized photon, nor a complex meteorological system, nor any of those things. I am just a guy thinking about which fork in the road I should take; and I want to have some assurance that the "me" that is "thinking"—which I believe corresponds in some complete and comprehensive way to the stuff in my brain—is actually making a real choice when I come to said fork in the road.

So when you talk about "the brain acting indeterministically", I see, of course, the logical necessity of saying that, since we've already painstakingly established that for it to act deterministically doesn't give us what we need. But I don't, in fact, have the slightest idea of what that actually means, what "indeterminism" *is* in this case. I only know what it ***isn't***.

So here, finally, is my question. Can you even imagine in principle an experiment which would be able to assess to what extent the brain acts deterministically or indeterministically? And relatedly, I think, can you imagine any experiment that might meaningfully probe what such a "brain indeterminism" actually involves?

AM: No, I can't. Maybe we'll get there in the distant future. Any indeterministic events are going to be small-scale events. They're going to be in a living brain. How are we going to get there and do these studies?

If, say, on the basis of brain scans, scientists could predict with a hundred percent accuracy which button the guy's going to press 10 minutes from now, I'd be quite impressed by that. But that wouldn't necessarily convince me that I could generalize to all decisions either, so one study like that wouldn't do it.

I think once we're down to that level, once we're down to the metaphysical level, whether you need determinism or indeterminism, we've gone beyond what we can study now.

HB: A good point to end on, I think. This has been a lot of fun, Al. Thanks very much for taking the time to chat with me.

AM: Same here. My pleasure, Howard.

Questions for Discussion:

1. Will we ever be able to prove or disprove that we have free will (in Alfred's mid-grade sense)?

2. Are you surprised that Howard, as a physicist, doesn't rely more strongly on the indeterminism of quantum theory? Do you agree or disagree with his scepticism that it might not significantly help us better justify free will?

3. To what extent does Alfred's work demonstrate a clear overlap between philosophy and psychology? How much of his research could, in principle, be done by those in a Psychology Department?

Continuing the Conversation

Much of this conversation was based on Alfred's books, *Free: Why Science Hasn't Disproved Free Will* and *A Dialogue on Free Will and Science*, both of which go into considerable additional detail about many of the issues discussed here. Two other related books by Alfred, *Aspects of Agency: Decisions, Abilities, Explanations and Free Will* and *Manipulated Agents: A Window to Moral Responsibility* were published after this conversation.

Ideas Roadshow Collections

Each Ideas Roadshow collection offers 5 separate expert conversations presented in an accessible and engaging format.

- *Conversations About Anthropology & Sociology*
- *Conversations About Astrophysics & Cosmology*
- *Conversations About Biology*
- *Conversations About History, Volume 1*
- *Conversations About History, Volume 2*
- *Conversations About History, Volume 3*
- *Conversations About Language & Culture*
- *Conversations About Law*
- *Conversations About Neuroscience*
- *Conversations About Philosophy, Volume 1*
- *Conversations About Philosophy, Volume 2*
- *Conversations About Physics, Volume 1*
- *Conversations About Physics, Volume 2*
- *Conversations About Politics*
- *Conversations About Psychology, Volume 1*
- *Conversations About Psychology, Volume 2*
- *Conversations About Religion*
- *Conversations About Social Psychology*
- *Conversations About The Environment*
- *Conversations About The History of Ideas*

All collections are available as both eBook and paperback.

www.ingramcontent.com/pod-product-compliance
Lightning Source LLC
Chambersburg PA
CBHW030903080526
44589CB00010B/123